Mary Cook

Liar, Liar, Pants On Fire!

Published by Creative Bound Inc.
P.O. Box 424, Carp, Ontario K0A 1L0
(613) 831-3641

ISBN 0-921165-40-4   Printed and bound in Canada

Book design: Wendelina O'Keefe

About the cover: Born and raised in Ottawa, **Brock Nicol** has been drawing and painting since he was eight years old, and has been a self-employed illustrator since 1987. Brock cites American illustrators Norman Rockwell and N.C. Wyeth, as well as Canadian illustrator Stewart Sherwood as artists who have influenced his work.

The original illustration on the cover is based on the story "Liar, Liar Pants on Fire!" (pg. 35) and is his latest collaboration with art director, Wendelina O'Keefe.

Canadian Cataloguing in Publication Data

Cook, Mary, 1932-

     Liar, liar, pants on fire

ISBN 0-921165-40-4

     I. Title.

PS8555.O566L43 1995   C813'.54   C95-900588-9
PR9199.3.C6394L43 1995

⫷ Dedication ⫸

I am truly grateful to the CBC and especially to producer Shirley Gobeil for giving me the opportunity to relate my memories and stories to a listening audience for so many years. And to the hundreds of people who faithfully continue to inspire me with their loyalty as listeners, I owe a great debt. I have been truly blessed with a supportive husband, Wally, and three patient children who over the years have accepted the fact that Mother sometimes had to be some place other than on the home front. They have weathered the storm beautifully and gone on to produce three adored grandchildren.

Many people have touched my life in a very meaningful way and in no small measure have contributed to whatever success I have achieved as a writer broadcaster. For the people of Renfrew County, and especially those from the Northcote area, I offer my sincere thanks for allowing me over the years to take literary license with their identities and personalities. And I thank God every day for bringing those folks into my life who have truly made a difference to me over the years.

To all of the people I have mentioned here, I humbly dedicate this book of memories.

Table of Contents

Introduction

I always thought my vivid imagination was one of my more positive attributes when I was a young girl in the 1930s. I believe my imagination worked like an insulating blanket. I could call on it at any time.

One of my most intense memories of my fantasy world was at meal time. Our meals were noisy and often argumentative, as brother was pitted against brother for the last sausage on the plate, or Audrey went into another plea for a permanent wave, or Mother and Father talked endlessly about the drought, or the rain . . . or cropping . . . or getting the chickens ready to take into Renfrew. My head would spin with the confusion, and there wasn't much room for the youngest and shyest of the family to be heard. I would look at the red and white checked oilcloth on the table, and the big glass spoon holder in the centre, and without even closing my eyes, I could picture myself at a long banquet table in some great and opulent home . . . before white damask linen, and pink flowered dishes, where the spoons were beside your plate with other gleaming silver. And I would be eating exquisite pastries and drinking wine from a crystal goblet. Only when Emerson would give me a sound poke in the ribs and shout, "She's dreaming again," would I be transported back to the old kitchen.

Another time of escape for me was in church. As our huge German minister droned on about the evils of man and how one day we would all die and go straight to hell, I would stare at a spot just above his head, so that no one would know I wasn't drinking in every word he said. And I would let my mind transport me into being one of the valley's most beautiful brides. Out of the corner of my eye I could see the aisle leading up to the front of the church and I could picture myself in flowing satin with a high diamond tiara on my head, and carrying peonies, my favourite flower. I could see the choir loft full for that day . . . and I could hear them in my mind singing love songs. I would remove old Mrs. Rummell from the front row, who always sang off key and cried through most of the hymns.

But try as I might I could never picture the face of the man I was about to marry. I could see in my mind's eye his tall frame and the back of his head, and his polished black shoes, but never his face. And I would stay locked in this reverie until a crash on the organ told me that we were ready to sing the closing hymn.

It would be hard for me to say what I miss most about being a child. I miss the sound of the crackling wood in the old Findlay Oval when my father rose at dawn to light the fire in the kitchen, and I miss the warmth radiating from the silver painted pipe that snaked its way through the upstairs hall and the back bedroom. I miss the smell of clean flannelette pyjamas that had spent the day in the frosty cold on the clothesline, and the hot bricks wrapped in the *Renfrew Mercury* at our feet in bed on a bitter night.

I long for the sound of fiddle music winging its way up the stairwell when we younger children could no longer keep our eyes open at the Saturday night house parties. Six or seven of us would lie crosswise on the bed drowsy from the late hour and the heat of the house, only to wake up mysteriously in our own beds the next morning.

I miss the smell of back bacon and scrambled eggs and seared bread toasting on the open lid of the cookstove on a rack when I came downstairs in the morning. And I miss seeing my mother standing at the stove in a sparkling white apron, called a pinny, stirring the porridge in the old blue granite pot.

I miss the simple joys of walking three and a half miles each way to school picking up friends at their gates as we passed along the Northcote side road. And playing jacks on the cement pump platform, and standing at attention each morning as we sang *God Save the King*, and the smell of lilac talcum powder when Miss

Crosby came to our desk to check our arithmetic.

And how I miss walking into our kitchen at night in fall and seeing jars of preserves on the bake table waiting to be taken down to the cellar for safe-keeping. And always there would be the bread-board with plum pits and Mother's own small hammer. I loved the pulp of the plum pits, and I would sit at the kitchen table and crack them open with the hammer and relish each morsel as I talked to Mother about my day at the Northcote school.

Above all, I felt sheltered from harm. If I had to choose, that would surely be my favourite memory as a child of the 1930s.

Two Left Feet

For several months, my older sister Audrey had been allowed to go to the church socials with Ralph. He was a big lumbering lad who lived on a farm several Renfrew County concessions over from us, and the dates, if you could call them that, were few and far between. Because Ralph wasn't allowed to drive the car, and it's doubtful Mother would have let Audrey go off with a boy in a car anyway, he would arrive with the horse and buggy or the cutter and I would stand with my nose pressed against the kitchen window watching him wheel into the yard and tie the horse to the fence.

When Audrey first started going out with Ralph she had been very excited. Emerson was the first to notice her interest was starting to wear off. He said it was because Ralph always smelled of cow byre. I said that was nonsense. We all smelled of cow byre.

And then came the week when they went off to a dance at the school. Audrey had borrowed Mother's velvet cape for the occasion and had put cornstarch on her face for powder. Mother said she was much too young to wear real makeup. She dabbed on some lilac cologne which we had bought for a penny at the Rexall One Cent Sale, and she went out the door with Ralph as happy as could be.

She was an entirely different Audrey when she got home. She said that was positively the last time she was going to a dance with Ralph. I was heartily disappointed, as I had already pictured her wedding with me as flower girl.

Audrey said simply, " . . . because Ralph has two left feet, that's why. And I'm never going to a dance with him again as long as I live."

Well, that statement gave me plenty to mull over in my mind. I had never heard of anyone with two left feet. I looked down at my brown brogues and wondered where Ralph bought his shoes. There was no doubt at all that I had one left shoe and one right one.

I glanced around at everyone in the room without saying a word. I had long since learned that asking a silly question, like how could anyone have two left feet, would send my brothers into a state of hysteria.

No, I would just have to find out for myself about Ralph and his two left feet.

He was to come for a game of Parcheesi on Saturday night, and I figured if I was ever going to find out about his deformity it would have to be then, before Audrey called it quits.

And so I laid out my plan in my head. Ralph came early that night. Audrey had already set out the Parcheesi board on the kitchen table, and Emerson was shaking the dice in a tin cup. Ralph hung up his coat on the hook at the back door and was sitting on the bench that held the wash basin to take off his galoshes. And I was right there at the ready. Without even asking Father's permission, I had taken his felt slippers from under the bed. I dropped to the floor beside Ralph and said, "Here, these will keep your feet warm." Ralph mumbled something about that being mighty nice of me, for it was obvious that I was going to put them on for him.

Both his feet were flat on the floor, and I sure took my time having a good look. They seemed perfectly normal to me. Well, I had gone this far; I figured I might as well settle the issue once and for all.

"Ralph, I have never seen anyone with two left feet before. Do you think you could take off your socks and let me have a better look?" Well, I certainly wasn't prepared for the scene that followed. Emerson rolled off the chair onto the floor in a fit of laughter. Everett and Earl got into a coughing spell, and Audrey was yelling for Mother at the top of her lungs. As for Ralph, he was stuffing his feet back into his galoshes and his face was as red as a ripe tomato.

He was out the door in jig time, never stopping to even say goodbye. Audrey was crying, and Mother had appeared to see what all the commotion was about. Emerson, who was always thinking of his stomach, finally regained his composure, headed for the cupboard, and said since we didn't have company any more we might as well finish off the sandwiches and the chocolate cake. ___

Warm Beds

Today, reflecting on the 1930s, I am amazed we didn't freeze to death in our beds, or at the very least have constant bouts of pneumonia. But Mother had ways of making sure that when we crawled between the two big, fluffy feather tickings the bed was warm and cozy.

There was no ceiling in the upstairs, just the high peaked roof, and the partitions in the bedrooms ended about where the roof met the walls. On a cold winter's day, you could lie in bed and see the frost making pencils of ice between the boards, even though Father had covered the inside of the roof with tarpaper, and then re-covered that with two-by-fours. It was still cold enough to cause hoar frost to appear, the very look of which sent chills up and down our backs.

One lone stovepipe snaked through the upstairs room and gave off a delicious heat as long as the log was fresh in the Findlay Oval in the kitchen, but as soon as it burned down we could feel the cold air seeping into the bedrooms, sending me burrowing deeper into the feather mattress.

We went to bed prepared for the very worst. Mother dreaded that the fire would go out and we would all be frozen in our beds when she got up in the morning. Consequently, we climbed between the feather ticking dressed like mummies. We often wore our underwear under our long nightgowns or pajamas, and I don't think I ever went to bed barefoot after the first of November. We wore Father's hand-knit socks, and on especially cold nights we were made to wear a sweater on top of everything.

Long before it was bedtime, Mother would take about six bricks from the back of the woodbox and place them on the top of the stove. For at least two hours they would absorb the heat to the point that you couldn't touch them with your bare hand without being burned.

Just before we climbed the stairs at bedtime, Mother would lift one brick at a time off the stove, using thick wads of newspapers for protection. She'd wrap the bricks in the *Renfrew Mercury* and climb the stairs, making several trips, until all the bricks had been taken to the bedrooms.

She'd thrust her hand between the ticking, placing the paper-wrapped bricks where she thought our feet would be. And by the time we got to bed, the bottom of the bed would be as warm as toast.

Just because the upstairs was freezing, we weren't excused from our nightly prayers, and we fanned out on the braided rug around Mother's knee. But before Audrey and I headed for the bed, Mother would run over and rub her hands briskly over the bottom ticking until she had taken the chill off the mattress. This exercise was reserved for my sister and me. The three brothers were not so privileged, and this to them was just another injustice heaped on them for being boys.

We had an all-purpose hot water bottle too. But it was only pressed into service if someone was sick. Mother wisely presumed that to give one out of five a hot water bottle would cause the other four to roar their disapproval until there was just cause to warrant the privilege. And I regret to say today that I sometimes tried complaining of a sore throat as I was tucked into bed, in the hope that Mother would fill the hot water bottle from the reservoir in the stove to put at my back. That ruse, however, backfired, for Mother felt anyone with a sore throat should also have a spoonful of coal oil mixed with honey and grated onion. Better to have a cold back than the traditional cure, I reasoned at an early age.

But the best bed warmer of all was surely my sister Audrey, who was much older than I, and therefore bigger. No amount of bricks, or hot water bottles, which always lost their heat in short order, could replace the feel of her back next to mine on a cold winter's night. She never once complained of my stockinged feet against her legs. And we'd be in bed only a short time when the wonderful warmth of that old feather ticking penetrated our bodies, sending comforting warm beams of heat through us. Our noses might be cold as ice, and frost might form on the roof, but our bed was as cozy as a nest.

The Woodbox

Every kitchen in Renfrew County had one. It was essential to the efficient running of the house, and though not terribly attractive, it gave the kitchen a finished look, and certainly fitted in rather nicely with the square box-like appearance of the Findlay Oval to which it was companion.

It was usually made of scraps of lumber. There wasn't too much attention given to the evenness of the boards, and there was no attempt to make it look like something other than what it was . . . *the woodbox.*

Through necessity, it was higher at the back than at the front, about a child's shoulder height. This allowed the young arms which were responsible for keeping it filled to bend over the lower boards at the front and drop the logs in with ease, and as it filled, to stack the wood high up the wall at the back and still keep it within the confines of the woodbox. It had a floor in it to keep as many of the scraps inside the box as possible, and our woodbox had a nail on the outside where the small shovel hung, handy for anyone whose turn it was to clean out the Findlay Oval of its accumulation of ashes . . . a job most of us detested with a passion.

Father always thought looking after the woodbox was an easy job, and it was delegated to the youngest of the household. In this case, the job fell to me, and I can remember wondering why Father thought it was such a cinch . . . I found filling the woodbox, a twice daily chore, a hard and tiring job.

In every season but winter, the wood was stacked in a lean-to at the back of the house, and although it was called the woodshed, it held many other commodities essential to the farm as well, such as a scythe, empty pork barrels, our sleighs, and an assortment of farm tools which wouldn't fit into the car shed or the barns. But in the winter, after the Findlay Oval was moved from the summer kitchen into the main part of the house, we five children took about three Saturdays in a row to carry in as much wood from the woodshed as the summer kitchen would hold. It would be stacked to the ceiling, just a step away from the main kitchen door, and this certainly made my job a lot easier.

Father was extremely fussy about how the wood was stacked both in the summer kitchen and the woodbox. We had to separate the large pieces from the small in the back kitchen, and when I was filling the woodbox, I had to be especially careful that the largest pieces were stacked on the bottom and to one side, with the smaller pieces and kindling on the top. And I had to leave enough room at the side so that the old copies of the *Renfrew Mercury* and the *Ottawa Farm Journal* could be squished down ready to use under the kindling in the morning.

Father would come in each night, go to the woodbox, lift a few pieces off the top to see that it was stacked just the way he liked it, and if it met with his approval he would simply nod in my direction. If it didn't quite measure up to his expectations, he would crook a finger at me, and I would have to unload the box, re-stack it, and then sweep up the pieces that fell to the kitchen floor. Father always said that if a job was worth doing at all, it was worth doing right . . . and by the time I was about eight, I was convinced I was the best woodbox filler in Renfrew County.

Some woodboxes were painted the same colour as the wainscoting that ran along the kitchen walls of most farmhouses . . . but Father thought that was sheer nonsense. It was a woodbox, plain and simple, and to try to make it look like something it wasn't was pretentious in the extreme. So ours remained in its natural wood state as long as we lived on the farm in Renfrew County . . . although I'm sure my mother would have preferred it to be painted green like the rest of the kitchen.

Because the Findlay Oval supplied the only heat we had in the house, I filled the box every morning before I went off to school, and it was the first job I tackled when I came home at night. Father kept a small ladder in the summer kitchen, and I had to climb to the top of it to reach the highest logs first and to keep the rows even . . . because I was small, I made many trips through the back door before I had the box filled. Occasionally, when there was no one else around, my older sister would run out quickly into the back kitchen, fill her arms with pieces of wood, rush into the house, and drop them into the woodbox to help me with my chore. But we were careful not to be caught, because Father also frowned on anyone doing someone else's job unless there was a perfectly good reason . . . like being confined to bed with pneumonia, for instance. But when Audrey helped me, I can remember how we would giggle and laugh at our bit of deception, and how grateful I would be.

I rarely came out of filling the woodbox unscathed. My arms would be scratched, I would have chips tangled in my long red ringlets, I would get splinters in my eyes, and many was the time I didn't quite make it to the woodbox, and the whole armful would crash down on a foot.

If Father was fussy about how the box was stacked, Mother was fussy about how the box was maintained. Every Saturday, it was my job to spread newspapers out on the floor, empty the box of any wood that remained, climb into it with the broom and the dustpan, and clean out all the pieces and bits that had accumulated over the week. As far as I was concerned, the woodbox got far more attention than it deserved.

The Bed Roll

There were only three bedrooms in that old log house in Northcote. Of course Mother and Father had one—the biggest of the three, my brothers had the back room, and Audrey and I shared one that was really a big hall at the top of the stairs.

We also shared a dresser. It was really a washstand, with two narrow drawers, and doors that swung open at the bottom. Audrey and I shared the double bed, which suited me just fine. On the coldest nights, her body was warm next to me, and if she fell asleep before I did, I would put my feet against her legs.

When a storm raged outside, I felt secure and protected because Audrey was beside me. And after the lamp was blown out at night, and the room turned to pitch black, I knew I would be safe, because Audrey was right there beside me, snuggled between the feather mattress and the feather ticking.

And then everything changed. It all started one Saturday when Audrey and I were doing our chores in the kitchen. This was a wonderful time together, that I loved. Audrey would set the bread and I would be allowed to punch it down in the big brown baking bowl. She and Mother would talk . . . and I would listen. Sometimes it was almost as if I wasn't there. But I didn't mind, because I was privy to what they were saying.

That day that I will always remember Audrey asked Mother if there was any possibility at all that she could have her own bed. She said she thought she was old enough to sleep alone and she nodded ever so slightly in my direction. Suddenly it was as though ice was running through my veins. Mother said she doubted it because there was no place to put two beds in the upstairs room we shared.

I was so relieved that the fear left me. But Audrey pursued the matter and begged Mother to find a place where she could put another bed. Again I was struck with a terrible fear. Audrey must have realized how I was feeling, because she said it wasn't because of *me* she wanted her own bed. It was because she was too old to be sleeping with a sister who was almost eleven years younger than she was. I'm afraid that did little to easy my anxiety. And I pictured in my mind all those nights when I would be terrified in the dark and when even the feather ticking couldn't keep the sound of the storms out of my ears.

I banged my fists into the big bowl and pounded down the bread as if it had something to do with Audrey's request. Then the subject was mercifully changed, when Mother nodded in my direction and said, "We'll talk about it later." And so I put it out of my mind, reasoning that if I didn't think about it, it would go away.

But after that terrible Saturday, I often heard Audrey broach the subject, and she and Mother would whisper so that I could only guess at what was going on.

And then one Saturday Mother got out the Singer sewing machine with the foot treadle and Audrey took the rag bag down from behind the kitchen door. She found an old flannelette sheet and ripped it in half. Mother sewed it down both sides, and neither said anything to me about what they were doing, but instinctively I knew whatever it was it was going to involve me.

Mother fashioned a long thin tube from the flannelette and Audrey stuffed it with clean rags from the rag bag until it looked like a long grey snake. Audrey seemed to be very excited. I asked Mother what they were doing and she would only say, "You'll see." And then whatever it was was finished; Audrey and Mother headed up the stairs with the fat tube and I was close behind them.

Because it was Saturday our bed had been stripped ready for clean flourbag sheets. When the bottom sheet was tucked tightly under the mattress Mother placed the long tube up the middle of the bed, and the bed roll was born. At first glance it was to me as if Audrey had built a fence down the middle of the bed, and I thought I was going to cry. But when she was sent downstairs with the used sheets Mother put her arm around my shoulders and said, "Now, isn't the bed roll better than two beds?" I thought of the alternative, and even though I knew in my heart that nothing in the world would ever be the same again, I also understood that the bed roll between us was Mother's way of separating an older sister from a younger one while still keeping us together.

Main Street

From early spring until late fall, or as long as the good weather lasted, it was a ritual in the farm community in the county, for those who were fortunate enough to own a car, to drive into Renfrew on a Saturday night.

You went in early enough to get a good position on the main street and there the car sat until it was time to go home around ten or eleven o'clock.

For the longest time when I was quite young, my sister Audrey would have nothing to do with me on these Saturday night trips into town. I was left sitting in the car, or else going into the one or two stores Mother frequented. Although there was plenty to see in these shops, I longed to walk the street with my sister.

She thought I was much too young. But after Aunt Lizzie sent me a little beaded purse where I could put my few pennies, removing them once and for all from the corner of my hanky, she began to think of me as being more mature, and agreed finally to let me go up and down the main street with her.

But she had steadfast rules by which I had to abide. I was to walk beside her, on the outside, since she being the older should have the privilege of walking next to the store window.

Audrey would be all dressed up for the occasion. After all, she was in the entrance class at the Northcote school, and mature young ladies in the 1930s wore their next-to-best clothes when it came to walking down the main street of Renfrew on a Saturday night.

This meant she had on her shoes with the little heels. I felt very young in my laced-up brogues, but I dared not comment, for fear of being left behind in the Model T in front of Thacker's garage.

That first night of walking together was just about the happiest night of my life. We met all sorts of country people we knew, and some even from the Northcote school. Audrey would smile and nod in their direction, and I soon took my cue from her and did likewise.

She said if we didn't dawdle too long, we could probably do both sides of the street before we had to head back to the car. One side was much better for window shopping than the other, however. All the stores I loved were located on the west side, whereas the other side had mostly office buildings and a few stores which held little interest for either of us.

"Now, this is where we start," Audrey said. It was almost like running a race, as we began our trip down main street precisely in front of Ritza's Drug Store. "And this is what we are going to do," she added. "We are going to pretend we can have one of anything we see in every window. And since I am the oldest, I will get first pick." That reasoning made absolutely no sense to me, but I knew better than to argue with Audrey. One word of objection and she was just as likely as not to head me right back to the car.

We would stop dead centre in front of every store window, and just as if we had the money right in our purses to make the purchase, we would pick something out of each window.

We loved the dress shops and Walker Stores. Even though there were usually children's clothes in the window, I always picked a very grown-up dress for my choice. Audrey picked just about anything that was red. The red purse, the red shoes, the big red bracelet in the jewellery store, and the red coat in Walker Stores' window. Since I was fond of red too, I was more than a little annoyed to find the best choices were gone by the time it was my turn to pick. I wasn't long in telling Audrey I thought this system was grossly unfair. I expected to be sent right back to the car. So I was thunderstruck when Audrey said, "Well, all right, we'll cross the street and you can have first pick in the next window . . . but only for that once . . . because I am the oldest," she explained.

We headed across the street right to a hardware store. There was a window full of cream separator parts, long bolts, hammers, chains, and a few galvanized pails. I looked over the window and couldn't think of one thing I would want to take home. Audrey told me to hurry up, or I would lose my turn. I finally settled on a set of glass bowls. Before I could complain, Audrey said, "There now, you've had first pick; I don't want to hear another word about it," and we headed back over to the other side of the main street, where once again I was relegated to the second choice position, and in front of some of the nicest stores in town. Life simply wasn't fair, I decided.

≈ Grandfather's Visits ≈

Grandfather's rumble seat car, I thought back in the 1930s, was a sure sign of wealth. And if the car wasn't symbol enough, his dress surely was. He wore fine grey felt spats and grey flannels and a navy blue blazer with a crest of the yacht club on the breast pocket. And when he rolled into the yard at Northcote the first thing I always noticed was the white silk scarf at his neck.

My mother's father spoke with an unbelievably soft French accent, and he would sing songs that he said his father had taught him. I could never pronounce the words, and when I tried he would throw his head back and laugh a wonderful deep laugh that seemed to come right from the depths of his gleaming white shoes.

He always brought us a bag of humbugs, and I never had the heart to tell him I hated humbugs with a passion. I would take one from the bag and thank him and tell him he was the best grandfather in the whole world. And then I would sneak the humbug into the nearest flowerpot.

In all the time Grandfather came to the farm he never brought what my father called farm chore clothes; he walked the barnyard dressed fit to kill, and of course that meant he couldn't lay a hand on a piece of machinery or a pitch fork or a milk pail. But that suited me just fine, because he didn't look as if he really belonged in a barn anyway. It also meant he could spend lots more time with me. Of course, he spent hours talking to Mother too. He would sit in the rocking chair in his flannels and a white shirt with the sleeves rolled up to his elbows, and the white silk scarf would be replaced with a polka dot ascot, which, I was assured by my sister Audrey, was the height of fashion.

When Grandfather came to the farm he always stayed several

days. And if I enjoyed the days when he was there, I enjoyed the evenings more. Because this was when Grandfather would sit in the parlour and we would all sit around him and he would tell us fascinating stories that would transport us to far-off places and introduce us to events that we had never before heard of.

He talked about playing lacrosse in a place called Cornwall, which he said had the best players in Canada. And he would get off his chair and make a sweeping motion to show us how he had scored against the losing team.

Or he would tell us stories about the Ottawa streetcars he helped keep in repair and about working under a big bridge where the traffic thundered overhead, and how he bought fish and chips wrapped in newspapers from a man with a horse and wagon parked on the street . . . "a whole batch for a nickel," he'd say, bringing the flat of his hand down hard on his knee, signifying that the price was something to be reckoned with.

When he talked about going to the "spots," as he called them, Mother never failed to raise an eyebrow in his direction. But she wouldn't dare ask him to halt his story. A "spot" was a beverage room over in Hull, where they served ice-cold beer in a big quart bottle and where his friends met to talk about lacrosse, and where the waiter brought little plates of crackers and pieces of fresh cheese.

Always one of us five children would ask him to tell us about what it was like living in a big city like Ottawa where streetcars roared by on tracks day and night, and about how the whole place would be lit up with street lights all at one time just because some man pulled a switch. And Grandfather would again tell us about the wonderful invention of electricity, and I would always ask him if he thought we would ever get it out to our farm in Renfrew County.

His eyes would sparkle and he'd tousle my hair and assure me it was just a matter of time. That no one could stand in the way of progress and, as sure as thunder, electricity was progress. And I would believe him with all my heart. Hadn't he said we would get a telephone and there it was on the wall by the back door?

When he thought it was bedtime Grandfather's stories would end abruptly. He would start to sing a French song . . . a familiar tune, but with foreign words, and we would climb the stairs filled to the brim with mind pictures of other places and exciting times. I would fall asleep listening to my mother playing the mouth organ and Grandfather singing. And I would feel bathed in the most wonderful warmth and contentment.

The Name of God

When I was growing up, I recall how affected we were by the presence of God in our everyday lives. It wasn't that we were fanatically religious . . . it was just that in those days believing in God was like having a built-in safety device that activated itself every time the need arose . . . and it was knowing deep in your heart that the Heavenly being governed every breath we took.

Now I remember, many years later, how God's name was worked into our everyday conversations as naturally as if we were talking about the neighbour on the next farm. His name was never taken in vain—in our house—but my father's speech was peppered with "by Gad's," which to us were too close to profanity for comfort. But since our mother allowed it, we children supposed it was all right, although we would never dare use the term ourselves.

But God was referred to under many circumstances. Our mother had a host of phrases, all relating to God's mercy. For instance, when Granny Hines died suddenly on the farm next to ours in Northcote, and one of the granddaughters came to tell us the sad news, I recall that Mother clutched her breast with her right hand . . . just about the vicinity of her heart, which to me added credence to the action . . . and in the most solemn tones said, "God rest her soul." At the time I had a great deal of trouble figuring out how Granny Hines's soul was going to rest if she was dead, but in those days you questioned not what was obviously a very serious statement. Thereafter I noticed that whenever my mother heard about a death, she went through the same routine of asking God to rest his or her soul. And once, when an absolute scoundrel died suddenly in the area—a man who had even stolen sheep from our very barnyard—I was astonished to hear my mother ask God for the same favour . . . I figured she was really putting Him to the test with that one!

God figured prominently in literally everything we did in those days, especially if we were contemplating an action in the future. For instance, we never said we would be going to the Renfrew Fair on Saturday; we always said, "We'll be going to the Renfrew Fair on Saturday, God willin'." I was young enough when I first heard the phrase to wonder why He would possibly object . . . but certainly we planned nothing down the road without adding as a safety precaution, "God willin'."

"If God favours" and "if God allows" were other phrases that slipped into my mother's everyday vocabulary too, and it was a frightening thing for me to realize that the reason she used the term was that there was some doubt in her mind as to where we would all be a few days hence, and to her the phrases made our chances of reaching that time just a little less risky.

"Only God knows" was a statement I grew up with, and it was used most often when my mother couldn't come up with a logical explanation for an action or circumstance. And so it was that the impact of that phrase literally governed our lives, because when I finally was old enough to absorb the meaning of the term "only God knows," I realized that absolutely nothing I could do escaped His scrutiny. I daresay that fact was largely responsible for the timid person I was as a very young child. I certainly wasn't going to take any unnecessary chances, for it was bad enough being found out by a parent if I misbehaved . . . I certainly wasn't going to tamper with someone as awesome as God!

But the reference to God which terrified me the most was found in a phrase an old German neighbour used frequently in our presence. She was a regular visitor to our Northcote farm and my mother often referred to her as "quite a gossip." I strongly suspect the woman knew her stories were often open to question, because when she told a tale, she would raise a fat arm high over her head, and with her hand cupped exactly like that of our Lutheran minister when he was giving the benediction at the end of a church service, and with her eyes closed, she would say, "If that isn't the truth, may God strike me dead." The statement sent chills scurrying up and down my spine, and I prayed fervently and silently that what she was saying was the truth, because I was sure that if it wasn't the absolute gospel, she would any minute go rolling off the chair into a heap on the floor . . . struck dead because of her lie.

When I look back to those days now, I realize it wasn't fear that prompted my mother into constantly referring to God's grace and asking his guidance, but an abiding faith. And in an era when there wasn't too much else to depend on, it isn't hard to understand why God was called upon so often.

Dreams of Splendour

Ithink I first began to fantasize when I got the big coloured calendar of the two young princesses to hang on my bedroom wall. Princess Elizabeth and Margaret Rose looked radiantly down at me in beautifully smocked dresses and they both wore little strands of pearls around their necks. I used to dream that I lived next door to them and that we would play together and share secrets and skip rope and play jacks. I had no idea where England was, but in my mind I would picture it as being just on the outskirts of Renfrew, a place I could easily get to, if the young princesses and I ever got to strike up a friendship.

I knew they were very important little girls, because certainly no one from Northcote school ever got to have *her* picture planted on a calendar from the cheese factory.

From then on, I found out how easy it was to dream. In the summertime I could lie in the hammock for hours, and in the wintertime I would stretch out on the couch in the kitchen, while my mind would take me to distant cities, and I would wear store-bought clothes and Mary Jane shoes that had never touched anyone's feet but mine.

And that's when I started to think if I talked about my dreams, just maybe they would come true. So I began telling my very best friend Velma that I was quite sure, if I had a mind to, I could become someone important, just like Princess Elizabeth and Margaret Rose.

Velma, who took every word I said as straight gospel, said she was quite sure I was right. And then I thought, well, if Velma believes me, maybe everyone at the Northcote school will believe me too. And so I settled on Marguerite . . . she would be the next one to hear my tale. Marguerite was easy to lie to. She always had so much more than I had . . . her clothes were store-bought, she owned a pony, had a permanent in her hair, and wore white stockings to school. Marguerite was everything I wasn't.

I picked the time carefully. It was at recess, and Miss Crosby had yet to ring the bell to summon us inside. Marguerite was squirming around in her new white rabbit fur coat with galoshes to match. I thought Princess Margaret Rose probably had a coat just like it. I chose my words carefully. "I got a letter this week." That was declaration enough . . . but I wasn't satisfied to let it rest there.

"It was from Princess Margaret Rose." Marguerite's big blue eyes grew to twice their size. "I don't believe you for one minute, Mary Haneman," she said. But I could see I had caught her attention. "I don't much care if you believe me or not," I shot back.

I was grateful when Miss Crosby appeared with the big brass bell. I probably would have forgotten about the encounter with Marguerite, but unfortunately for me, *she* didn't forget about it. She rushed right home, told her mother, and the two of them were at my house before dark to see the letter from Princess Margaret Rose.

I am not quite sure how I lived through the new few minutes, but I do remember Mother saying something about there being a misunderstanding, and shooing them out the door to the cutter. The tears came before the back door was closed. And I remember to this day being rocked by the cook stove as I poured out my fantasies to my mother.

I was so sure I would be sent to bed without my supper for lying. But instead Mother told me that it was all right to have dreams and fantasies. That she had them every day. She dreamed of going back to New York . . . she dreamed about singing on the stage on Broadway. And she told me that the only thing I had to remember about dreams was that it was best to keep them to myself, unless I could really make them happen. And *then* it was all right to talk about them.

Well, I never did get a letter from Princess Margaret Rose, and as long as I lived on the farm, I rarely had store-bought clothes. But that didn't stop me from dreaming, because then I knew it was all right . . . hadn't my mother told me so?

Liar, Liar, Pants on Fire!

It didn't start out to be a good day. First of all, we were almost late for school. And that was because our Uncle Lou was visiting us from New York City. It was always hard to break away from our very favourite relative, and that morning we had dallied and said our goodbyes a dozen times and listened for just a few minutes more to his tales of that wonderful romantic city that we knew we would never see. But finally, we were out the door and ran almost the full three and a half miles to the Northcote school, arriving just as Miss Crosby was about to ring the old handbell on the step.

At recess, of course, everyone wanted to know why we the Haneman children were almost late, since we were usually just about the first ones to arrive. I blurted out that our very rich Uncle Lou was visiting—you know, the one with the big black Buick car, and the one who always brought bags of fruit with him from the city . . . and in case they still couldn't place him, I reminded everyone that this was the uncle who was putting a marble floor in the Empire State Building.

We had been learning about the Empire State Building in school and I was consumed with pride over the fact that we had a relative who had even a remote link to this wonderful building more than one hundred storeys high.

It was Marguerite who brought me up short. "I don't believe for one minute, Mary Haneman, that you have a relative who has been anywhere near the Empire State Building, let alone one who is working on it. Besides," she added, "Miss Crosby said the building is finished, so what would your uncle be doing putting a floor in it now. Liar, liar, pants on fire!" she yelled at the top of her screechy voice.

As usual I was mortally wounded over the attack. Whereas my brothers and sister just ignored her, I took everything Marguerite said to heart, and I went home feeling lower than I had ever felt before.

My mother had a wonderful ability to determine when something was wrong with any one of us. She read me like a book, and I was soon telling her how I had made a fool of myself talking about Uncle Lou, and that Marguerite had planted doubt in everyone's mind that he even existed, let alone that he had anything at all to do with the Empire State Building. Mother said little. But she patted me on the head and told me not to worry, that everything would work out just fine . . . wait and see, she said with a big wink.

But that night I went to bed with a heavy heart, dreading school the next day. Uncle Lou came upstairs and tucked us into bed, and for a time I put Marguerite out of my mind, but I went to sleep dreaming of the hateful girl riding in the front seat of Uncle Lou's big black Buick.

Mother, Father, and Uncle Lou talked late as they always did when he came for his visits, and the next morning Mother said we wouldn't be walking to school that day, that our uncle would be driving us. So we sat around the breakfast table laughing at his jokes and loving every minute of the extra time at home.

We all piled into the big Buick and roared out the lane, down the Northcote side road, and right up to the gate at the school. But instead of just leaving us out of the car and heading home, Uncle Lou got out and took a cardboard box from under the seat and walked tall and straight with me by the hand right up to the door. Miss Crosby was obviously expecting him, and she ushered him in as if he were a member of the Royal Family. She explained that Mr. Lapointe had called her at her boarding house last night, and since we had been reading about the Empire State Building in the *Farm Journal*, he was going to talk to us about it.

"He's the Hanemans' uncle, you know," she said. I glanced over at Marguerite, who was beet red and squirming in her seat. Uncle Lou went to Miss Crosby's desk and put down the cardboard box. I have no idea exactly what he said, but he talked about the world's tallest building and how he was building some of the marble floors and then he said, "In fact, I have some pieces of that marble with me, and I thought each of you would like to have a little bit to keep." He asked me to take the box around to each desk. I almost passed Marguerite's without stopping, but decided against this cruel deed. I glared at her as she reached in and looked for the biggest and shiniest piece.

Then, after shaking hands with Miss Crosby, he was gone. I knew then that Mother had asked Uncle Lou to come to the school, and I knew why she had done it . . . and at that moment I loved her more than I ever had in my whole seven years of life. ~~

The Red Wagon

There was no doubt in anybody's mind that Mother was pretty much the decision maker in our family back in the 1930s. It wasn't that Father didn't have a mind of his own. On looking back, I think he mulled over a situation with such deliberation that Mother's impatience would get the better of her, and she would end up making the decision for him.

Father accepted this situation with tolerance, even though I could tell he would often be disappointed if a decision was made without his consent. But I also knew that Father's mild and passive personality preferred the line of least resistance.

There was one time in particular that Father tried to press his preference onto Mother. It had to do with the simple issue of painting the driving wagon red.

Both Father and his sister Aunt Lizzie loved red. It was always somewhere on Aunt Lizzie's person. Father had to resort to a red cotton handkerchief only, since Mother couldn't stand the colour. Perhaps one of the reasons for her dislike of red was that Aunt Lizzie wasn't one of her favourite in-laws.

At any rate, that year Father casually mentioned at the breakfast table that it was time to paint the driving wagon, and instead of the coat of black paint it usually got, he thought this year he would use red.

I immediately glanced at Mother. She stopped midway between the Findlay Oval and the table. "Now Albert, you know how I hate red. And that wagon really suits black, I think . . . with the double seat in black hide and all. Besides, red would be so outstanding parked in the yard of the Lutheran Church . . . so obvious. No, I think it should stay black."

Father put his fork down and chewed silently for the longest time. "No, I think this year I would like red." Mother wasn't going to let the issue die there. "Now, Albert, we would be the only ones on the Northcote side road with a red driving wagon. Now that in itself wouldn't bother *me*. But I know how you hate to be conspicuous. So let's give it a nice new coat of black paint." Our heads turned from Father to Mother as if we were watching a tennis match.

Mother thought the issue had been laid to rest. But Father, we could tell by just the way he was holding his jaw, wasn't going to give up without a fight. And he didn't. He went on about how he couldn't understand why Mother didn't like red. It was a perfectly nice colour, as far as he was concerned. He fingered his red and white handkerchief which he had removed from his overalls pocket.

I personally would love to have had a red driving wagon. Everyone I knew in Northcote had theirs painted black, and I could think of nothing nicer than driving to the Northcote Lutheran Church on Sunday morning in a bright red wagon. I was hoping Father would pursue the matter. But Mother announced it was time to "red up" the kitchen. As far as she was concerned, the discussion was over.

Father was the last to get up from the table. He stood by his chair for a few moments. "Seems mighty strange to me, it does," he said in a low voice, "how a man can work from dawn to dark and not have a wagon the colour he wants."

I noticed Mother pause. She watched Father grab his hat off the nail at the back door and head to the barns. She stood looking at the closed door for the longest time.

Since it was a Saturday, she shooed my sister Audrey and me upstairs to start the cleaning, and announced that she would be heading into town to get the week's supplies . . . and no, we couldn't go, there was too much to do around the house.

It was a long drive into Renfrew with the horse and buggy, and Mother didn't return until late afternoon. We five children helped her haul the supplies into the house—the bags of flour and sugar, five pounds of green tea, some new print from Walker Stores for fresh aprons. There was also a closed cardboard box which she insisted she carry herself. Emerson said he knew it was going to be the black paint for the driving wagon. She went into the kitchen and put it right on Father's chair at the kitchen table, where he would be sitting for his supper.

When he came in, hot and tired from a full day in the fields, Father washed up in the basin at the back door and went straight to his chair. He opened the box and lifted out the gallon of paint. It had "red" written on it in big black letters. Mother never looked up from the frying pan. Father looked at it and then looked at Mother. Nobody said anything for the longest time. Mother finally broke the silence.

"It seems mighty strange to me," she said, "that a man who works from dawn to dusk can't paint a wagon red if he wants to." All of us, including Father, threw back our heads and laughed.

The Easter Bunny

Emerson knew how much I loved my little white rabbit. Everyone I knew called their rabbit Thumper, but I called mine Prettyface, which my hateful brother said was just about the silliest name he ever heard of for a rabbit.

My pet was very tame—in fact, Father often said Prettyface thought she was a dog, because often she slept in the doghouse when old Sport wasn't curled up inside. But I was the only one who could actually pick her up. Her favourite position was lying upside down in my arms, with her four feet high in the air, and her ears lying down over my hands like pink handkerchiefs.

That Easter I remember so well, Emerson said he doubted if Prettyface would make it through the holiday. He said he had been offered a whole dollar by an old bachelor down the Northcote road if he could come up with a rabbit for his Easter Sunday dinner. And since it was just about impossible to snare a rabbit when the snow was gone, he figured Prettyface would fit the old man's bill to perfection.

I went howling in to Mother, who told me to pay Emerson no heed. She was sure he was just trying to upset me. Well, he did that continually, and with little effort on his part. But the week before Easter I kept a keen look-out for Prettyface.

Emerson said that dollar was looking better and better every day, and he'd rub his hands together and run an eye over my beautiful rabbit, obviously with murderous intent in his heart. My every waking hour was spent chasing down my pet to make sure she was still alive.

Easter Saturday broke clear and warm. Just the kind of day Prettyface loved. She would sit on the back step and sun herself, and she would allow me to pick her up and scratch her ears. I went out the back door to look for her, but she was nowhere to be found. I searched the doghouse and the grape arbour where she sometimes went to sleep. I called her and whistled through my teeth, which always brought her hopping in my direction. She was gone.

By this time I was frantic. I ran to look for Emerson. He wasn't as elusive. He anticipated my move, and he met me head-on at the cow byre door.

"Looking for something, are you?" I told him he knew perfectly well what I was looking for, and if Prettyface didn't surface immediately, I would personally take his scalp off one hair at a time.

He took a clenched fist out of his pocket. "Never had a whole dollar before. Sure feels good," was all he said. I leapt on his back and grabbed him around the neck with a death grip. But I was no match for my hulk of a brother, and I was soon looking at the rafters in the cow byre.

All day I searched the barnyard. I whistled and called and looked under steps and even went as far as the west hill. Prettyface was nowhere to be found. By bedtime, Emerson was still showing off a clenched fist, where he assured me his dollar bill was secure. I was heartbroken, but resigned to the likelihood that my hateful brother had sold my rabbit to the old bachelor down the road.

I had no heart for the egg search on Easter morning. Emerson wore the most hateful smirk, and Mother kept insisting that Prettyface was just off wandering somewhere. But I knew in my heart she was gone forever.

I pretended to search for our homemade Easter baskets with my sister Audrey. I half-heartedly looked under the beds and in the woodbox for the hard-boiled eggs and the butterscotch penny sucker the real Easter bunny left us every year.

Our search took us to the back woodshed. I looked in the woodpile. Nothing. Audrey and I went outside. Under the back steps was a box, the kind we brought groceries in from Briscoe's General Store. The Easter rabbit had scratched my name on the box with a pencil. I half-heartedly pulled it out and opened the lid. There was a flash of white fur, the sound of scratching feet, and there was my beloved Prettyface.

I knew no Easter bunny had put my pet in a box from Briscoe's General Store. It had to be my hateful brother. I was raging and happy all at the same time. My rabbit was alive, but at the same time, I made a solemn vow that I would plot my brother's demise as soon as possible.

At that moment he surfaced from around the corner of the back shed. I made a bee-line for him. He had in his hand my real Easter basket with my name on it, held high over his head. Just then Mother appeared at the back door to announce that breakfast was on the table. Emerson handed over the basket as meek as a lamb and said he was just holding it for me.

It was too long a story to tell Mother of my two-day ordeal. No, I figured my best revenge was to lie in wait for an opportunity when I would do Emerson in, on my own terms. ━

Touched by Human Hands

I have always thought the most exciting time on the farm was in the late winter or early spring when new baby pigs arrived. I would stand at the doorway of the barn and see these little pink bodies appear, perfect miniatures of the big old sow whose only acknowledgment of this exciting event was a loud snort now and then. She seemed much more interested in the bucket of mash she always got when the task of delivering her new piglets was over.

Father had steadfast rules for us when baby pigs were born. He was the only one allowed near the operation, and the reason he gave was that the mother would not accept her babies if they were touched by human hands.

For some reason which I cannot explain to this day, the piglets on our farm were always born on a cold damp morning. I can remember shivering in the doorway of the barn; the door had to be left open to provide enough light for Father. This made the barn drafty and damp, and there was always the worry that the piglets would get chilled after they were born, and succumb to pneumonia.

So it was that as each one emerged, it was lifted gently with a bran bag, Father being especially careful not to let his hands touch the newborn. He would wrap the baby pig in the bag and rush into the house. Mother would be ready for him. The oven door of the old Findlay Oval would be down, and lying on it a big fat cushion covered with another bran bag. The piglet would be gently transferred from the carrying bag onto the pillow. Behind the stove, which stood out from the wall by a good two feet, would be a wicker hamper filled with straw, and as Father brought in the next baby, the last one would be moved to the basket.

This process went on until all the little pigs had been born and treated to a warming session on the oven door and then transferred behind the stove.

I remember the year I raced back and forth from the barn with Father, never once laying a finger on a piglet. I adored the little silky pink animals, and so wanted to hold one. However, Father's warning of abandonment by the old mother kept me from reaching out and lifting one from the cushion or from the wicker basket.

Mother was caught up in the job at hand as well. Grown pigs fetched a good dollar, to say nothing of the food they provided for seven hungry mouths on the farm . . . a fact I refused to think about. There was much scurrying about as the piglets arrived fast and furiously. Mother and Father were running either in or out of the kitchen, moving the little ones to or from the oven door. I was simply a spectator in this farm drama.

But I wanted to be more. I told Mother I thought I was quite capable of moving the pigs from the oven door to the basket. She said no, because if we touched them, the mother wouldn't take them back.

"You heard your father . . . you can watch, but you can't put a finger on them. Besides, I think we're just about out of little pigs." She was heading back to the barn. I looked at the little pink creature on the oven door with a black spot on one ear, squirming and trying to burrow into the bran sack. I thought it was the most beautiful little animal I had ever seen.

And right then and there a thought formed in my mind. So what if the mother pig didn't want her baby back. Hadn't I raised a black lamb all by myself? I tried not to think of the terrible end it had come to. Unknown to me at the time, we had eaten it over the course of one winter. I eased closer to the oven door. I swear it looked up at me. All reasoning went right out the window. I could feel the heat of the Findlay Oval on my face as I bent close to the pillow.

And then I did the unthinkable. I reached down and picked up the little silken body and put it up to my face. It squealed and burrowed its head into my neck, and right then I didn't care if I was sent to reform school, which is where we all thought my brother Emerson would end up one day. But Mother would be coming through the door any minute, so I quickly parted with the little pig, gently putting it into the basket.

"I was sure there was one still on the oven door," Mother said as she breezed into the kitchen. I never raised my head. That night after supper Father and Everett carried the basket out to the barn and, using the bag, lowered the piglets one by one down to the sow. I never took my eyes off the one with the black spot on its ear . . . waiting for its rejection. The old sow grunted and fell to her side. The thirteen piglets found their nurse, including the one with the black spot on its ear.

I never had the courage to tell Father how I knew his theory on mother abandonment didn't hold water.

New Curtains

Spring cleaning was as important to my mother in the 1930s as preparing the land for planting was to my father. This was the time when the braided rugs were cleaned and rolled in newspapers, walls washed, floors scoured, and the windows cleaned with vinegar and water. And every year as long as I can remember, Mother went through the same exercise of standing back, appraising the home-made flourbag curtains and vowing that this year they had to go. But when the house cleaning was done, and the curtains taken down, washed, starched, and ironed, Mother would sigh and say they didn't look all that bad, and she guessed they'd do for another year.

That is, until the year she washed them and, before she had a chance to touch the iron to them, they fell apart. They came in off the fence, where they had been stretched out to dry, in long ribbons. Instead of showing any sign of despair, Mother actually looked pleased, and she announced to Father at the supper table that night that this was the year she was finally going to replace the kitchen curtains.

Father reminded her that he needed a new set of harness, and had she forgotten that when he put the Model T up on blocks last fall there were only two tires worth holding over the winter? Mother said she didn't care, and that she would find the money someplace, but by the end of the week there would be new curtains, store-bought ones, hanging in the kitchen window. "And you can count on that, Albert Haneman," she said with defiance.

We knew the blue sugar bowl was empty. She had cleaned it out to buy seeds at Scott's hardware store the week before. And there was not much hope of increasing the number of eggs our hens laid every day, especially this time of year. That night she browsed through Eaton's catalogue, but decided she didn't want to wait for the mail order to come in. No, she would have to buy them at Walker Stores in Renfrew on Saturday. None of us knew where this money was going to come from . . . and at the time, we honestly didn't think Mother knew either. But she always said God would provide. Audrey and I wondered if His charity extended to something as frivolous as kitchen curtains.

Mother hummed most of the week, while glancing at the bare kitchen window and measuring with string and making notes on the back of an envelope. Father stopped asking where she thought the money was going to come from. "Blue checked. Yes, I think I would like blue checked . . . you know, large gingham," she would say to no one in particular, and she would stand back and look at the window just as if the curtains were already there.

Mother never paid much attention to the mail. It was always Father who stood waiting on Mr. Kallies and his horse and old buggy to come down the side road. But that week Mother was always at the gate waiting when the mailman came around the bend in the road. The week was passing with nothing more than the usual collection of bills. Mother seemed not the least concerned.

On Friday, as she had been doing all week, Mother walked to the gate with us to wait for the mailman. We could hear the clop, clop of the horse rounding the corner. After their greetings Mr. Kallies handed Mother the mail. We five children hung around. We were always excited and amazed at letters that came from outside Renfrew County.

"Ah, a letter from your Uncle Lou," she said as she tore open the envelope. This was Uncle Lou from New York . . . with the big Buick car, who bought fruit when he came to the farm. Inside was a letter and a five-dollar bill. Mother just nodded as if it was an everyday occurrence to get a letter with a five-dollar bill in it.

"It's for my birthday," she said. We said we never knew Uncle Lou to send anything for her birthday before. She agreed, but said she felt all along that she would be getting some money in the mail.

"I wasn't sure who it would be from, but I knew it would come. Plenty here for those kitchen curtains . . . and some left over for a piece of material for the front door, too." She turned and walked back to the house.

"Mighty strange," Emerson said. "Pretty funny," offered Everett. "Eerie," said Audrey. I didn't find it strange at all, knowing Mother.

～ A Lesson Learned ～

My mother had many ways of teaching her young children lessons in the 1930s. And she never missed an opportunity to lecture her charges on what she considered important issues of the times.

I can no longer remember how the subject came up that Saturday morning. Mother and I were working alone in the drive shed. I hated the job we were doing, but I uttered not one word of complaint, because this time shared alone with my mother was time I cherished very much. There never seemed to be an instant when one of my brothers or my sister weren't around, all of us vying for Mother's attention. And here we were alone in the drive shed on a Saturday morning, filling pillow casings with feathers. And as was always the case, I was talking non-stop. There were so many things to talk about to Mother alone, and I didn't want to waste a minute.

Mother was a wonderful listener, and I often think today that she devised alone time with each of her children so that we could unburden our hearts to her when there was no one else around. Of course, she was also a great believer in the work ethic, so this was not a time when we simply sat and talked . . . this was chore time, as well.

As always, I spilled my heart out about bad Marguerite, who aggravated me at the Northcote school and made my life miserable every chance she got. And as always, I got carried away with my tales of her misdemeanours. I became quite taken with my story, in fact, and the more I talked about Marguerite, the more colour I put into my tale.

Mother was taking in every word, nodding at the appropriate time, and raising an eyebrow when the occasion merited it.

I was getting right into the spirit of the telling, and I could see no reason, since I had such an intent listener, not to embellish my story as I went along. Finally I was ready to reach the climax, but I thought I might just as well throw in one last affront. I stopped stuffing the feathers into the pillow case so that I could get the most effect from my statement.

"And I hear she steals too. Right out of Miss Crosby's desk," I added for good measure. Mother asked me whom I had heard that from. I hedged for a second, and then I said, "just around." Of course, I hadn't heard anything of the sort. In fact, Marguerite had lots of faults, but in my heart I doubted she would really steal. Mother asked me if Marguerite's honesty had ever been questioned. I said it probably had. But when she asked me by whom, I was hard pressed to come up with a name. "So it probably isn't true," Mother said.

And then she did a very strange thing. Taking one of the feather-filled pillow cases she beckoned me to the outside of the drive shed. I followed her around the corner to the back, where there was a small slope in the yard. There was a good breeze, and Mother clutched the top of the pillow case in her hand. Our skirts billowed in the wind.

Mother opened the pillow slip and burrowed her hand deep into the soft feathers. She raised her arm high above her head and I watched, not knowing what she was doing. Then she opened her hand and the feathers got caught up in the wind and blew every which way in their lightness.

She turned to me. "Can you get back those feathers?" she asked. Not one was within a dozen yards of the back of the drive shed. I assured her retrieving the feathers would be an impossible task.

She rested a hand on my shoulder. "You see how those feathers have spread? They are gone goodness knows where. You can never get them back. They are gone forever."

I tried my best to understand what Mother was trying to tell me, for I knew there was a lesson there somewhere.

"That's what the spoken word is like," she said. "Once it is released, it can never be taken back. And when you say something about someone, yes, even someone you are not very fond of, you have to be awfully sure you are speaking the truth." We watched the feathers . . . gone beyond reach.

"And that's what a rumour is like, you know," she said. "It is just like those feathers. Once it is released, it can't be put back." She turned with the pillow slip in her hand, and we both walked back into the drive shed. I had learned a lesson and we had a job to finish.

⚛ Pots ⚛

Mother was known to take the clothes off our backs before they had absorbed the warmth of our bodies and toss them into the laundry tub. Father said she took this cleanliness business far too seriously, but even he had to admit that the day my cousin Daisy came to the farm to spend a week, Mother's desire for sanitation was justified.

The spring cleaning had been accomplished and there were few remnants around to hint of the winter just over. Heavy clothes had been packed away, the rugs rolled up and put under the beds, and the windows washed with water and vinegar. And once the warmer weather was here, even the chamber pots from under the beds were scoured and put away until fall. Mother really didn't think they were very hygienic, but they were the best alternative to going out in the freezing night air to the outside privy in the dead of winter.

She always insisted that each chamber pot be covered while in use. And so each night we put a heavy magazine or newspaper over the top until it could be emptied in the morning. We thought this an unnecessary gesture, but Mother thought it was more sanitary. Father thought it was nonsense.

By early May we were forced to abandon the chamber pots, and then had to make nightly treks out to the privy, which scared the starch out of me. But Mother said chamber pots were out of the question in warm weather, and one Saturday my sister Audrey and I were told to collect them, take them out to the back yard, scrub them, soak them with Javel water, and let them dry in the sun. Then they would be stacked in the chimney cupboard upstairs, after being wrapped in the *Renfrew Mercury*, to stay until the first chill of fall descended on the old log house.

Audrey and I had done our hateful task. The pots were scoured and brought into the house, and lined up on chairs in the kitchen waiting to be tucked away. It was then that Uncle John arrived in the backyard with our cousin Daisy. We all liked Daisy, but she was a "bubble off plumb." She didn't go to school, even though she was Audrey's age, and had frequent outbursts of hysterical giggles for no apparent reason. She came to the farm because Mother thought it was good for the young girl. And she loved to work in the garden, or feed the calves, or help in the kitchen. Mother insisted anyone who could set a proper table and weed a garden wasn't a lost cause, and that one day, with the proper training, she would be able to look after herself. Mother always found little jobs for Daisy to do, who worked better on her own than with someone watching over her shoulder.

So it was that on the day she arrived, Mother asked her if she would like to peel the potatoes and carrots for supper. Daisy was overjoyed, and the rest of us vacated the kitchen to let the girl work on her own.

Mother let a goodly time pass. We had picked up sticks from the yard and taken them to the brush pile; we washed the milk pails; we filled the water bucket at the pump. Mother guessed Daisy would be finished by then. As we headed towards the door we were regaled by the sounds of Daisy's singing off-key and the loud clatter of dishes. We guessed she had decided to set the supper table.

I will never forget the look on Mother's face as we went into the kitchen. There was Daisy . . . with the most contented look on her face . . . small curls of golden hair hanging down her forehead, her big white pinny wet to the knees, and two chamber pots full of peeled potatoes and carrots. I thought Mother was going to be sick right there on the floor. She was careful not to alarm the girl, who was overjoyed with the job she had done. Mother simply thanked her for peeling the vegetables, trying not to look at the chamber pots sitting up on the cupboard—a position they had never enjoyed all the time we lived in Renfrew County.

Mother suggested I take Daisy to the swings in the grape arbour, just as Father was coming in the kitchen door to wash up for supper. He saw the vegetables . . . he saw Daisy with the paring knife . . . he saw the chamber pots on the cupboard. He could read the situation as if it had been spelled out on a blackboard. He put his hat back on and headed out the doorway to the barn.

We all knew supper would be late that night, and we all knew the pigs would be getting an extra treat in their evening mash.

Wild Strawberries

For some reason, my three brothers were never asked to pick wild strawberries. That job always fell to my sister Audrey and me. Oh, the brothers often picked them for their own eating, but when it got down to the serious business of picking the strawberries for preserving, or to serve at meals, it was Audrey and I who were sent out to do the job.

The berries grew in great clusters along the railway tracks which laced through our farm. The tracks were a distance from our old log house, and I was always frightened when it came time to head out with the honey pails. As far as I was concerned, it was too far away from home, and once we were over the west hill, I could no longer see my mother in the kitchen window.

My brother Emerson, who could be hateful at times, said he knew for a fact that some children went as far as the tracks and never came back. Of course, when he was asked for names, he couldn't come up with any. But once he had planted the idea in my head, it remained there forever.

Father had to cross the tracks to go to our back fields, and he was the one who informed Mother that it was "pickin' time." The honey pails came with little wire handles back in the 1930s, and when empty they became berry pails, for Audrey and me to put the berries into. But we had to carry a larger pail too, so that we could empty the little honey pails into it.

Loaded down with the two honey pails, and a milk bucket, and lunch wrapped in a flourbag tea towel, we would head back to the tracks on a Saturday morning. We left the house early to enjoy the cool of the day's beginning, but by noon hour we would be sweltering in the heat, and I would have eaten most of the lunch and downed all but a smidgen of the lemonade.

And all the time Audrey and I would be lamenting the unfairness of life, that sent us back to the tracks to pick berries while the brothers stayed home and did barn chores.

Neither Audrey nor I could abide snakes. Before we started to pick in a patch, Audrey would take a switch and beat the grass to make sure any that might be loitering there would be shooed away. Emerson had told us snakes were especially fond of wild strawberries.

That Saturday we arrived with our pails and Audrey found a switch and cleared the area of whatever might be hiding among the berry plants. We could never agree on whether it was wise to pick quickly and finish the job in jig time, or stretch the chore out and so avoid housework when we got home. That day we decided to take our time.

We spent about two hours picking, and Audrey had lamented that the berries seemed smaller that year. The milk pail was far from full. I suggested we finish off what was left of the lunch.

There wouldn't be another train over the tracks for at least a few hours, and so we balanced the bucket on the centre ties, and Audrey and I sat on the rails with our feet in the stones in front of us. There wasn't a sound except for the crows circling overhead, hoping we would drop a few berries for them. Suddenly Audrey's voice stabbed through the silence like a butcher knife cutting bread. Audrey could scream louder than anyone I knew. She pointed to the rail across from us. There was an enormous green grass snake inching along the tracks as if its main mission in life was to devour us in one bite. We jumped from the rails and were half-way across the field before you could say berry pail. We hit the fence at the same time. "We forgot the berries," I panted. Audrey said she would give me her new lisle stockings if I would go back for the pails. I weighed her offer carefully in my mind and decided the stockings weren't worth it. We debated going home and saying there were no berries, but then we would have to explain our two-and-a-half-hour absence.

There was nothing to do but go back to the tracks. Audrey said to pick up stones on our way and make an apron of our skirts to hold them. She said there was no time to explain. When we got within a dozen feet of the tracks, Audrey began tossing stones towards the spot where we had seen the snake. We inched our way ever so slowly, scanning the site as we went. There was no sign of that hateful critter. We grabbed the pails and roared back towards the fence as if our lives depended on it.

After that we tried to negotiate with Mother that the boys would pick berries and we would do barn chores. She would have none of it.

Emerson, of course, took full advantage of our experience. He said it had probably grown to twice its normal size too. He said it was just a matter of time before it tracked us down and had its revenge. As far as I was concerned, Emerson was telling the gospel truth.

The Mysterious Order

Mother was feeling very pleased. It wasn't every day that a chicken customer phoned a farmer, looking for fowl. Usually our chickens were sold only by rapping on doors as we went up and down the side streets in Renfrew. But that week a woman phoned from town saying she would like Mother to deliver two fat chickens the next time she was in town. Mother said that would be Saturday, and would the woman be interested in a dozen sticky buns and maybe a dozen fresh eggs at the same time? The Renfrew woman would be delighted.

Immediately suspicious, Father said that anyone who phoned for chickens at the height of the Depression was probably a dunner. What with every farmer in the country trying to peddle his crop door to door and all, there were plenty of farmers to choose from, and why would she pick someone way out in the backwoods of Renfrew County?

Mother said he was born with a suspicious nature, as she set the buns on Friday night and the boys went to the henhouse to pick out two fat chickens for the one-way trip into town the next morning. As was usually the case, I was allowed to go into Renfrew on Saturday morning, where Mother's routine rarely varied. First she would deliver her wares. Then she would sit in the Model T on the street behind the Walker Stores, count the money, and when she was sure she had enough, she would head for the store to fill her list.

That day she planned on heading right for the address on Raglan Street that the woman had given her over the phone. It was over a store on the main street, one of the many apartments occupied by older people in the 1930s. Mother said she knew exactly where it was.

We pulled into the curb at the appropriate spot. Mother handed me the sticky buns, and she carried the eggs and the chickens. I was thrilled to be involved in this new kind of transaction. Mother gave a loud rap on the door leading to the second floor. There was no answer, and after a few minutes she decided we would just go in and up the stairs.

We could hear loud voices and I could hear music, probably from a victrola, I thought, which led me to believe this customer must be rich.

Mother rapped at the door at the top of the stairs. It was promptly opened by a woman in a Salvation Army uniform with a hymn book open in her hand and her mouth open in song. It didn't take a genius to figure out we had walked in on a prayer meeting. Everyone stopped singing as the woman pulled Mother and me into the room, which was set up like a sparsely furnished hall. An old pump organ sat in a corner and the woman in full regalia on the organ seat swung around and gave us a wide grin of welcome.

Another woman reached out for the sticky buns. The one who greeted us at the door was oohing and ahhing over the chickens, which were wrapped in one of our best pillow cases. She was saying how wonderful it was of Mother to bring all this food for the needy of Renfrew, and wondering how she knew the meeting was to gather sustenance for those on welfare in the town. I was always infatuated with the Salvation Army uniform and I thought the gathering was just about the smartest group of Christians I had ever laid eyes on. We were being invited in for prayers, but Mother took me by the elbow and we practically ran down the stairs, unencumbered by eggs, chickens, sticky buns, or money.

Mother was so exasperated she had to sit on the step outside the building to compose herself. I knew she was wondering how she could have been so mistaken in the address of the woman who had phoned. I wondered if we should just go up and down the street rapping on doors. Mother pointed out we had nothing to sell.

By the time we were a few miles outside of Renfrew Mother had completely resigned herself to our loss. She said there wasn't that much on her list which couldn't wait until next week, and maybe the mystery customer would phone again. And by the time we got to Briscoe's General Store at Northcote she felt pretty good about her unintentional good deed. So good, in fact, that we went into Briscoe's and Mother ordered a full pound of bologna, ten cents' worth of cinnamon gum drops, and a bag of maple cookies. And she said to Mr. Briscoe: "I'm a little short this week. Please just put it on my bill." As we climbed back into the Model T, Mother said she could see no reason for Father to know what had transpired in Renfrew. I heartily agreed. ~

≈ Blue Bloomers ≈

Being allowed to take off our long underwear for the very last time in the spring was a joyous day for me. But because Mother lived in constant dread that I might, through neglect, come down with pneumonia, the summer was almost here by the time I was allowed to shed those hateful navy blue fleece-lined underpants.

Once we got rid of the long johns, and to keep our skin from turning blue from the dye, we wore homemade flourbag pants under the navy bloomers. I could see no earthly reason why I had to wear two pairs of underwear to school when the snow was all gone. And my little friend Velma Thom felt exactly the same way. The fact that bad Marguerite had long ago shedded her navies didn't help matters in the least.

By the time we reached the corner leading down to the Northcote school, we would have met up with several more students and we would walk together for that final two miles of rutted, washboard road. Velma and I, being the youngest, paired off, and we were pretty well ignored by the older pupils.

One day, when the sun was especially warm on our backs, I suggested to Velma that we should slip in behind the cedar bushes and remove the navy blue bloomers, put them in a secure place on the branches, and on our way home put them back on—no one would be the wiser.

Velma thought that was the best idea she had heard in a long time. The schoolyard was in view, and a quick look told us Miss Crosby was nowhere in sight. No one seemed to be looking when we slid down into the ditch, came out at the log fence, and slipped through the rails to the other side.

We rolled the fleece-lined pants into a ball and tucked them into the lower branches of a tree, then raced on to school like two colts being let out of a barnyard for the first time.

Cecil said he saw us go into the bushes and wanted to know what we were up to. Velma told him to mind his own business. It didn't take us long to spread the news that we didn't *have* to wear our navy blue fleece-lined bloomers any longer. We made it sound as if our mothers had made the decision, and we lifted our skirts to show off a stretch of bare leg and the elastic edge of the flourbag undies.

All during the morning work period, Velma and I would exchange warm friendly glances as if we belonged to some secret club. The seat of our desks felt cool and smooth.

Recess came and we ran into the yard feeling ten pounds lighter than usual. Neither of us saw Cecil. We heard the commotion first. He was running through the schoolyard like a reindeer. He had two branches high in the air. Everyone was laughing hysterically, and we had to leave the cement stoop where we were playing jacks to see what all the fuss was about.

Well, we couldn't believe our eyes. The sticks were V-shaped at the ends, and attached were Velma's and my navy blue fleece-lined bloomers. As he ran at breakneck speed, the underwear stood out like two flags. He passed one of the branches over to Two-Mile Herman and the two of them came within inches of our noses as they circled the yard again.

Velma and I were so horrified that we both blurted out that the bloomers didn't belong to us, which only added to the certainty that they did.

Miss Crosby emerged with the bell, just as Cecil was taking another cut around the school. She grabbed him by an ear, and Two-Mile Herman had the common sense to walk up to her and hand her the other branch as if it were a gift, saying Cecil had given it to him.

We weren't above lying to Miss Crosby if the situation merited it. But since apart from Marguerite we were the only ones in the whole school without navy blue bloomers on, it didn't take the teacher until four o'clock to figure out who owned the underwear. We were sent to the outside privy to put them back on. Velma said if we could just figure out how to do it without being caught, we would be perfectly justified in murdering Cecil.

Discipline 1930s Style

In our household a parent's word was the law. The punishment for disobeying depended not only on the crime, but also on the parent who was to administer the discipline. If we had to be disciplined, we much preferred Father to mete out the punishment rather than Mother. Father was considered soft-hearted when it came to his children, whereas Mother felt a disobedient child would never amount to a hill of beans, and so her reprimands were usually quick and, on occasion, severe.

Rarely did we five children get into trouble at the same time, but I do remember one Saturday when we did stray from the hard and fast rule of obedience.

It was late May or early June. Mother and Father were both going into Renfrew for the week's supplies, and they decided there was too much to do around the farm for us children to go with them. The potatoes needed to be planted, for instance. It was a job we hated desperately. It was back-breaking work. Water to saturate the hills had to be dragged from the pump in the back yard all the way to the potato field, which was a goodly distance by our standards. Mother said it was a job five strapping children should be able to handle with ease, as she climbed into the Model T beside Father, leaving my older sister Audrey in charge. And she expected the planting to be finished by the time they returned.

It was a hot day for that time of year and by the time my three brothers had dragged the potato bags over to the field, Audrey and I following with the spades and hoes, we were pretty nearly done in.

We used to plant a lot of potatoes on our farm. They were a dinner staple back in the 1930s. And what we couldn't sell door to door in Renfrew, and what we couldn't eat ourselves, were cut up into pieces and fed to the pigs. Nothing was wasted.

Of course, we had to plant them first, and that was the job at hand that day in Renfrew County. Everett thought we should just rest a bit before we got into potato planting. None of us could see a thing wrong with that suggestion. Emerson said we should run across the next field and have a quick dip in the Bonnechere. It would only take a minute. We could go in our underwear and it would soon dry out in the sun. Audrey, who was much older, had no intention of going into the river in her underwear, but she could see no harm in the rest of us doing it if we so wished. But we'd better just be quick about it, or Mother and Father would be back and the job we had been given would be staring us in the face.

Well, I don't have to elaborate on what transpired. The river was so inviting, it was so awfully hot in the morning sun . . . before we knew it, the morning was gone. Everett said we should stop for lunch. Audrey asked, "stop what?" We hadn't done a lick of work. We were just putting the last piece of bread into our mouths around the kitchen table when we heard the old Model T coming in the lane. We didn't even wait to wipe up the crumbs. We headed for the potato field as fast as our legs could carry us.

It didn't take Mother and Father all afternoon to figure out we hadn't done a tap of planting. Father sucked on his pipe, and mumbled something about how we'd never make farmers, and set to digging holes with the hoe. Mother wasn't going to let us off so easily. She told Father we would just have to be taken to the woodshed and dealt with. For some reason which I cannot explain to this day, the woodshed was always the place we were sent to be dealt with.

Father said it was awfully hot and you couldn't really fault us for wanting a dip in the river. Mother said that wasn't the issue. We had not done a job we were supposed to do, and Father might just as well get his task over with. Father kept on digging. Mother said if he didn't tend to the discipline right away, she would. We all knew what that meant, and wished Father would put that hoe down and pay attention to the more pressing job of straightening out his children. Mother's threat to take things into her own hands finally convinced Father he had better do as he was bid.

He herded us into the shed while Mother took to the hoe. We were far enough away from the potato field that she could not hear what, if anything, was going on inside the lean-to. After closing the door, Father went over and sat on a wood horse and lit his pipe. He dragged on it to get it going while we shuffled from one foot to the other. After several minutes had passed, he got up and walked to the door and said, "All right, now . . . you've been dealt with."

But when he got close to the potato field his voice grew louder and he pointed his finger and his pipe at each of us in turn. Giving us each a big wink, he said, "Now, let that be a lesson to you." Mother seemed satisfied that the proper discipline had been meted out in the proper fashion.

Team Work

I f someone had asked me what it was I didn't like about Marguerite I would have been hard pressed to come up with a definite answer. There was no doubt I hated her because she had a white fur coat and she was only seven. But she had other traits too, which rubbed my skin like a piece of sandpaper. Take the spelling bee, for instance.

To this day, I have no idea how she managed it, but she always seemed to fidget her way to the first of the line, and so got the easiest words to spell. Or at least, so *I* thought. And then came the news to the Northcote school that the local Board of Education was having a spelling bee for the whole area. Our school was to be pitted against Admaston.

Well, let me tell you, I couldn't wait. Those snooty Admaston kids always had their noses in the air. They lived across the Bonnechere, and did they ever think they were something! We'd show them.

For days Miss Crosby drilled us on spelling. We even had to give up our story book at half past three in the afternoon, which the whole school looked forward to with great anticipation. But this was serious business. It was the first time we ever went outside the school to compete with *anybody*, and Miss Crosby wanted to make awfully sure we were up to the challenge.

The only problem with the whole idea was that awful Marguerite was to be at the head of the line. I seethed inside like a dog with a sore paw. I couldn't imagine why Miss Crosby didn't see right through her. But there she was, every day, standing up along the side of the schoolroom with her back to the blackboard like she owned the place.

I kept waiting for her to make some glaring mistake. But her mother must have kept her up all night going over every word in the speller, because that hateful Miss Snooty never missed once.

And the day of the big event was coming ever closer. Miss Crosby arranged and rearranged the line a dozen times. The strong spellers were put at the front of the line, the passable ones in the middle, and ones who were likely to blow the whole contest at the end. I was fortunate enough to be close to the head of the line.

And even though I wanted our school to win, I would have loved to see Marguerite miss every word thrown at her. I knew I was evil to have those thoughts, and I even considered adding my confession to our nightly prayers around Mother's knee before we went to bed, but then I would really be in trouble . . . not only with God, but with Mother as well.

And so the big day rolled around. We were all dressed in our best clothes. For me that meant my navy pleated skirt with a hand-me-down blouse my sister Audrey had worn years before me. Marguerite came, of course, looking like one of those paper brides on the top of a wedding cake. The Admaston children were driven to the Northcote school by their parents, who were invited to stay for the spelling bee. And there was Marguerite, dancing around like she owned the place. The inspector rang the bell and we all took our places, lined up like two rows of cornstalks, facing each other across the schoolroom.

The words started out simple and got harder and harder as the contest continued. Marguerite never missed a cue. And only when the half-time bell rang did she finally misspell a word, but Velma, next in line, picked it right up. The Northcote school was ahead by a country mile.

Well, I thought Marguerite was going to explode. Twice Miss Crosby had to raise her finger in her direction, which was all Miss Crosby had to do to get immediate action. And then it was over. The Northcote school got a long red ribbon, handed out by the inspector, and the Admaston school got a blue ribbon, and everyone went home happy as a clam. That is all except me. You'd swear

Marguerite had won the contest all by herself. And I wasn't shy about voicing my opinion either.

Well, I guess I had taken my contempt a little too far to suit Mother. When we got home she sat me down on the bench at the table. She asked me the silliest questions I ever heard of. Like what were Father's favourite horses. I said King and Queen. "A team, right?" I agreed and wondered where this conversation was taking us. "And you know the men who were here last week to cut wood; why do you think they got so much done? Because they were a team . . . they worked together." For the life of me I couldn't understand what all of this had to do with bad Marguerite and the spelling bee. But then Mother zeroed in for the kill. "Now, how do you think the spelling bee would have gone if only you were up there against the Admaston school . . . or only Marguerite, for that matter?" Well, it didn't take me any longer to figure out what she was trying to tell me. "Do you see how it takes a team working together to accomplish many things in life?" I was getting pretty uncomfortable, so I said yes. The lecture was over. But when I went to set the table for supper, I couldn't help wondering why bad Marguerite couldn't have been on someone else's team rather than mine.

⇜ Softball ⇝

I always hated it when we had to choose sides at the Northcote school. I hated when two people were chosen to be captains, and they alone made the decision who was going to be on what team. Be it a spelling bee or a ball game, I found this method of determining sides both humiliating and nerve-wracking. I probably felt this way because I was very shy and I lived in constant dread that I would just never be picked.

I was a good speller, but I was a terrible ballplayer, and so I found the choosing of teams for ball even more terrifying than choosing for the spelling bee. And this time of year it became a well-established fact who the best ballplayers were in the Northcote school, because the warm days saw us out every recess warming up and getting in lots of practice for the time when the Douglas school team would meet up with us for a final game in late June.

One year I remember particularly. A young girl had moved to the Northcote area just a month or so before school closed. Like me, she was very shy, and she hung back and generally kept to herself. No amount of effort on Miss Crosby's part could loosen the girl up, and she frequently had a look of sheer terror on her face. The fact that she was enormous, I'm sure now, contributed greatly to her shyness. She wasn't tall, but she was almost completely round. To add to her appearance of ample girth, her mother put her in dresses that came below her knees and cut her hair in a short bob with straight-across bangs. This made her face look like a round plate. The boys made fun of her at first, always behind Miss Crosby's back, of course. But they soon tired of that sport when their interests turned to ball practice.

Then came the day when Miss Crosby said that *everyone* in the school would play ball, or there would be no more playing at recess. Today that would cause roars and groans in the classroom, but no one, not even the most strapping of farm boys, would dare contradict Miss Crosby back in the 1930s.

And so at recess, under the watchful eye of our teacher, two captains were appointed, and the choosing process began. It goes without saying the best-known runners were chosen first. That was just about every boy in the Northcote school!

The captains looked over the culls left huddled in a corner of the schoolyard, mostly girls terrified of not being picked, and terrified of the alternative. The new fat little girl, who had never even set foot on our ball field, was among them. And then she was the only one left. Cecil let out a huge sigh, which could be heard all over the yard, and motioned her to join his team.

Miss Crosby also insisted every one of us have a turn at the bat. I would have been just as happy if she had left well enough alone. The fat girl and I were on the same team. It didn't take long for one of the big strapping Kallies boys to strike me out. The ball never came within a foot of the bat. And then it was the new girl's turn at home plate.

She had tucked her skirt into the elastic of her navy blue bloomers, which was more than I would have done. She took a stance just like one of the big Briscoe boys from the side road. She was sure observant, she was! She tested her swing a few times, pawing the air with the bat, as if she knew exactly what she was doing. And then she nodded to the pitcher. She let the first one pass over the plate, and Miss Crosby yelled "Strike!" I was really feeling sorry for her, and knew that even if she did hit the ball, her chances of getting to first base without being tagged out were pretty slim.

Then there was this crack that shattered the Northcote air like a bullet. The ball arced towards the dirt road, and the bat landed somewhere near the back door of the school. The fat girl took off like chain lightning. I had never seen anyone run so fast in all my life. It took the outfielders forever to find the ball, which had come to rest in the tall grass outside the schoolyard. By this time the batter was standing at home plate, having covered the three bases in less time than you could spit.

Cecil was the first one to recover. "Holy smackers," he hissed. Miss Crosby was beaming and calling for the next batter. It didn't take long for everyone to realize we had a first-class ballplayer on our team. Miss Crosby let us play until the new girl had one more turn at the bat. Her repeat performance cemented forever her acceptance at the Northcote school.

But her emergence as a fine ballplayer didn't come without its price. Every day there was a battle royal between the captains as to who would have the new girl on their team. Miss Crosby devised a long and complicated process, having to do with numbers in a hat, to determine who would have first pick. And the look of terror disappeared forever from the new girl's face. ~

✸— Horsebuns —✸

I think now, so many years later, the only reason my brothers felt such animosity towards Marguerite was because they knew she didn't rate very high on my list of friends. I tolerated her, but if the truth be known, I was as jealous of her as could be, with her bottled Shirley Temple curls, her little pony, and her white knit stockings and patent leather shoes.

Besides, she was the only one in her family, which meant she never had to wear hand-me-down clothes. It also meant she had no one to play with on a Saturday, and it was obvious she didn't have to do chores either. I always worked through a list a mile long, and usually managed to finish by noon hour, leaving the afternoons free. And that's when I could count on Marguerite being driven to our farm by her mother. Emerson suggested I could hide in the hayloft if I didn't want to play with her, but I knew perfectly well my mother wouldn't tolerate that kind of behaviour. I would just have to make the best of a bad situation.

School had been out about three weeks, and Marguerite never missed a Saturday coming over to our farm. Emerson said he hoped she wasn't planning on a weekly visit right through until September. My sister Audrey said she couldn't imagine why he was concerned; she wasn't coming to see him. "That's for darn sure," Emerson retorted.

And then came the Saturday when the visits were brought to an abrupt and unpleasant halt. It was a warm muggy day, and the sun was just above the house ready for its steady decline over the west hill. Marguerite had pranced out of her mother's buggy in a sparkly white dress with blue ribbons and those hateful Mary Jane shoes and short white stockings with lace around the tops. I looked down at my overalls, bare feet, and a cotton gingham blouse Mother had made out of an old housedress. I wondered what Marguerite saw in me. And I also wondered how we would ever wile away a whole afternoon. Her mother didn't stay around long enough to find out. Had errands on the Northcote side road, she hollered . . . she'd pick up Marguerite late in the day. Emerson could be heard groaning from the corner of the summer kitchen and Everett and Earl were in a huddle beside the rain barrel, planning goodness knows what.

It was Everett who suggested we play Ball Over the Roof, which was one of my favourite pastimes. Marguerite and I would stand on one side of the summer kitchen and the three brothers on the other. We would take turns tossing the softball up over the pitched roof and letting it roll down the other side. The trick was to throw it over at a different spot each time. If and when you caught the ball, you yelled "score" and the next person took a turn.

Emerson yelled, "You catch first, Mary." I waited for the ball to come over the edge . . . not sure just where it would surface. It bounced over and down our side and I caught it with ease. "Score," I hollered, and prepared to send it back. "Score," I heard Earl yell. And then it was Marguerite's turn to catch. "Here it comes!" Everett yelled.

We saw it surface at the crest of the roof. The bright sun almost blocked it out . . . but that Marguerite was a smart one. She moved closer to the summer kitchen right under where the ball was sure to land. Her arms were outstretched and her face was skyward. It was coming slower than usual, and Marguerite was ready. It landed in her cupped hands and then she roared like a banshee as it broke into a million pieces and covered her from her neck down. It didn't take me long to figure out what she had caught. The boys— no one ever admitted which one it was—had taken a not-too-old horsebun, rolled it in white lime, and headed it over the summer kitchen roof. To this day I have no idea why I yelled "score!" It just came out of me.

It took Mother the better part of an hour to wash and iron the white dress, and of course Marguerite had to have a good scrubbing too. The brothers were dealt with in the usual fashion . . . sent to bed early without their supper.

When my sister Audrey and I finally climbed the stairs that night, the three boys were still snickering in the back room. When I finished saying my prayers, Emerson said a loud Amen. Everett said he reckoned we wouldn't be seeing much of Marguerite for the rest of the summer. Earl yelled, "score!"

The Grape Arbour

Back in the 1930s the grape arbour served many uses, and I am not sure now if Father worked the vines to form the arbour, or if they grew that way naturally . . . although I strongly suspect Mother had asked Father to coax the long vines into shape. Natural or otherwise, the grape arbour was a high arch of green leaves, completely closed in on the north, east and west sides, with only the south portion, facing the old log house, open for easy access.

I used to think the hollow was enormous. As big as our kitchen it was. And Father and Mother could easily stand up inside the arbour, so it would have had to be a least six feet from ground to the top vines.

As soon as the leaves formed, the hollow was immediately turned into an outdoor room. At the start of the summer season the grass inside was thick and green, but after a couple weeks of constant use, the grass shrivelled up and died and left a soft mat of straw in its place.

Mother would move a washstand into the very back of the cavity, and Audrey and she would take enough dishes out of the kitchen cupboard to stock the washstand for the season. A bake table from the summer kitchen, two benches from the drive shed, and the big wooden swing with the double seats—and the grape arbour was ready for business.

We still ate our breakfasts in the house, but unless it was pouring rain our noon meal was eaten outside. Father tried to tell Mother using the grape arbour as a dining room added to her workload tenfold, but Mother always said it was worth the effort. We carried the food out on trays covered with sparkling white tea towels which remained on the steaming bowls and platters all the time we were eating. Heaven forbid that a fly should come within a country mile of something that was going into our mouths!

It didn't matter how hot the day, the grape arbour was always cool inside. The big flat leaves kept the hot rays from penetrating, and if there was a breeze, they still allowed the air to circulate, so it was a most pleasant place to spend an hour at noontime.

Father, instead of going into the kitchen to the creton couch, would tilt back an old weatherbeaten chair against the table and have his mid-day nap, which he seemed to be able to slip into with the greatest of ease inside or outside the house.

When the meal was over Audrey would bring out the big white granite dishpan filled with hot soapy water, and even the clean-up from the meal was done outside. Sport, our old collie, stood at the ready, waiting for whatever morsel was left on a plate. No need for a dog dish outside.

On Saturday morning, as a rule, the grape arbour was off limits to everyone but my sister Audrey. Her best friend Iva Thom would come to visit, after each had done her chores, and with their embroidery work or knitting they would head for the old wooden two-seater swing. I was never allowed to go near them. Mother said they had earned a time of privacy. How I longed to listen in on their grown-up talk about boys and spooning, and kissing, and goodness knows what all . . . subjects which I knew for a fact peppered their talks in the grape arbour. But they kept their voices low, and the big green haven sheltered them from young prying ears and the world outside.

When I was given the privilege of having the grape arbour to myself, I would take my dolls out there, and the cavity would become my house. I would rearrange the benches to form rooms, the table would be the bed, and I would slip into a world of fantasy where I alone had admission.

I often think of the grape arbour. I think of the quiet times I spent there with my mother, she with her sewing basket on the ground at her chair, me sitting beside her listening to tales of her life in New York City before she moved to the farm in Renfrew County. And I would think there was no better place to be in the whole wide world than in that most secluded of spots, the grape arbour.

Fool Proof

Father was sitting with his feet propped up on the oven door. He had his chair tilted back, and the door was simply a steadying device, so that he wouldn't tumble backwards and break his neck, which Mother predicted regularly was one day bound to happen. It was a blistering hot day, but Father still wore heavy grey knitted work socks, and his laced boots sat beside the straight-back kitchen chair like two obedient dogs waiting for the call of their master.

His glasses, which he had bought at the Five-to-a-Dollar store in Renfrew for seventy-five cents, were sitting on the end of his nose, and he was reading the *Family Herald and Weekly Star*, which he favoured over the *Ottawa Farm Journal* at noontime.

Then something struck his fancy, and he was out of the chair in one leap and over to the kitchen table where we were dawdling over the last crumbs of a big chocolate cake Mother had made that morning. He jabbed his pipe at a square advertisement that appeared in the upper corner of the paper. "Read that . . . right there. By gar, that's what we need on this here farm, and by the holy thunder I'm going to send for it!" His fist came down with such a bang that he rattled the dishes on the table.

"In fact," he said, "I'm going to send for two of them." All of us rushed over to the end of the table—even Mother, who knew it had to be something special to get Father to spend a dime on anything other than the bare necessities of life.

The ad was about four inches square. Guaranteed to kill your potato bugs, it said. Absolutely foolproof. Send one dollar for this amazing kit.

Well, if there was anything we all hated on the farm it was

killing potato bugs. And because they seemed to come to our potato plants by the thousands, every last one of us was pressed into service. It was a laborious and backbreaking job. Father would fill honey pails or old baking powder tins half full of coal oil, and we went up and down the rows popping the bugs into the cans. And God have mercy on you if you missed a bug, because Father went up and down the rows after you to make sure the job was done to his satisfaction.

Mother agreed that anything would be better than picking off the potato bugs and popping them into tins of coal oil. Father went to the sideboard, took down the blue sugar bowl, and drew out two one-dollar bills. Audrey was ordered to address the envelope. Father personally put in the two bills with his name and address written on a piece of paper, and Emerson was dispatched to the mailbox at the end of the lane.

Father said that for the next few days *he* would look after fetching the mail. He was just beside himself with excitement, and said he couldn't wait to get his hands on this wonderful invention that was going to end forever one of the most hateful jobs on the farm.

In those days it didn't take a month to get a letter out west and a return answer. So in less than a week Father retrieved a small parcel from the mailbox, and headed right for the kitchen. We were as excited as he was.

Audrey fetched the scissors, and Everett offered to cut the string. Inside was a plain brown cardboard box. Father lifted the lid. He took out four pieces of board about six inches square. Two pieces were tied together with more string and a sheet of instructions was anchored to the top.

Father turned the boards over in his hand. Then he asked Audrey to read the instructions. She read, "Untie the string. See small circle drawn on one of the boards. Place potato bug on circle. Bang other piece of board on top of bug in circle."

That's all there was to it. Father scrounged around in the box to see if anything was missing. No one said a word. Father took a match out of his pocket, scratched it on the leg of his overalls and lit his pipe. Then he lit another match, went over to the Findlay Oval, and touched the match to the paper and kindling that were always at the ready. He walked back to the table, picked up the box, paper, and the four pieces of wood, took them over to the stove, and fed them into the firebox.

He turned on his heel and headed for the door. Not a word was spoken. All of us rushed to the window. We saw him at the drive shed filling the small tin cans with coal oil.

On the Mower with Father

I don't suppose Father thought any more of me than he did of my three brothers and my sister Audrey. But it seems to me now in retrospect, I was sometimes given special favours when I was a child on our Renfrew County farm.

Father was a simple man—uncomplicated, straightforward, and honest. We had only to look at him to know if he was mad or sad, as Mother used to say. He wore his disposition on his face. And I think the times he was the happiest were when he was working his land.

Ours was a big farm by today's standards—one hundred and fifty acres of tillable land and bush, with big sprawling fields and gentle hills. Father often walked his property from one end to the other, just for something to do, he would say. But I think now it had more to do with pride and the fact that his great grandfather had cleared the fields and built the stone fences and planted the trees along the lane to the Northcote side road.

This time of year he was usually far from the house, back in the fields that were west of the Bonnechere river. Here he would cut hay and grain, crossing the shallow bed with the horse pulling the piece of machinery through the water and up over the west bank without benefit of bridge.

And Father would be gone for the whole day. It was too far, in his estimation, to come back to the house for noon dinner, and so I was allowed to take his lunch back to him in a big eleven quart basket. It was a time I treasured, and still do to this day. But one day I remember in particular. It was something that I thought then set me apart from my brothers and sister where Father was concerned.

When I arrived at the field with the basket of lunch, Father was sitting on the big iron seat of the mower, cutting the hay and oblivious of his youngest daughter standing in long grass waiting for him to come full circle.

And then he saw me. As always, his pipe was hanging in his mouth. His old straw hat was pulled down to protect his eyes. He acknowledged my arrival with a nod . . . nothing more. I had already picked out the tree we would be eating under. It was just outside the field, and there was nice soft grass around it, and a spot for old King to munch. I had brought him some green apples I had picked off the tree on the way through our backyard.

Father stopped the mower right in front of me. There was no 'hello' . . . nothing in his face to say that he was glad to see me. Then he crooked his arm and motioned me to come closer to the mower. I found a place for the basket of lunch, climbed over the pile of stones that served as a fence of sorts, and walked over, the mowed hay filling my nostrils with the smell I loved so much. I got to the mower and stopped. King turned his head to look at me. He would sense, I felt, that I had a treat for him tucked into the leg of my flourbag bloomers. Father put his hand down, and only then did he smile. He was inviting me up on the iron seat beside him. He said he thought I might like to ride around the field a couple of times. Father always cut hay from the outside in—our neighbour cut his from the inside out—so I knew it would be a wonderful long ride. He moved his small bony frame over in the iron seat as far as it would go, and I scrunched my haunches in beside him. My feet stuck out like sticks and I had no place to hang on to. I wasn't sure I was going to like this after all.

He clucked through his teeth and King jerked ahead with the mower. I watched in horror as the see-saw of the big blades started to cut the hay, and I wondered how many feet we would go before I tumbled down on top of them. But I need not have feared. Father circled my body with his free arm, pulling me tighter onto the iron seat, telling me to hang onto his braces. And there we were, the two of us, bumping along over the rough field of hay, making two complete circles before Father brought King to a halt under the big tree. He still hadn't said more than a dozen words. But I knew in my heart there wasn't one of my three brothers or my sister who would have been given a ride on the mower.

We ate the lunch in silence and, as I was heading back over the fields, Father said not to tell Mother I had ridden the mower. "For some reason, she's scared to death of these things," he said. And he gave me a big wink as he slapped King's flanks with the reins. ━

The Mortgage Man

To this day I have no idea why I believed all the stories Emerson told me. But he had a wonderful ability to make everything credible. And so is it any wonder that I believed him with my whole being when he told me that one day the mortgage man would be coming out to get me.

He said this evil man lived in the bank. Well, I certainly knew where the bank was in Renfrew, but I also knew Mother and Father had no money in this big building. Every cent they owned was in a blue sugar bowl on the bottom shelf of the kitchen cupboard. And so I questioned, with my knees knocking together, why this man from the bank in Renfrew would be even remotely interested in *me*. Emerson said it was because Mother had borrowed money and she was having trouble paying it back, and when that happened, as it often did during the Depression, Emerson said the banker simply came out to the farms and took the youngest child in the household.

I said I thought he was lying. I asked him what on earth the banker would want with me. I was only seven. I wasn't clever like my sister Audrey, and I was certainly too young to do much housework. Emerson said that didn't matter in the least to this most evil of men. He would train me to do housework, and I would have to stay there until the debt was paid off. He said, too, that I wasn't to mention a word to Mother, that she was worried enough about the money she owed the bank, without having to worry that I had found out what was in store for me if she couldn't pay it back.

And so every time we went into town for our supplies, I would find an excuse to walk past the bank. I wanted to get a look at this man who was about to alter my life forever. But the windows were high, and I was never able to get as much as a peek at him. Emerson said he drove a big black car. "Looks much like a hearse," he said. And that revelation sent even more shivers up my spine.

Then one day the phone rang. Two longs and a short . . . our ring. The banker was the farthest person from my mind when I picked the receiver off the hook. I listened to the deepest voice I had ever heard asking for my mother. I said she was out gathering eggs. And then he asked me if I would give her a message. Well, I was good at that. I couldn't write well, but I had a good memory, and Mother often said I took the best messages in the whole house.

And then the voice said something that sent ice through my veins. He said, "Just tell your Mother it's the banker, and I'll be out on Saturday." I will never forget the fear in my heart, as I counted off the number of days I had left to live on the farm at Northcote. I briefly toyed with the idea of not telling Mother at all, but gave up on that idea when I considered the alternative.

The most amazing thing to me was that when I told Mother when she came in with the basket of eggs all she said was, "Finally. I thought he had forgotten. Saturday, you say; are you sure?" She was so calm I couldn't believe it.

The week went by so fast, just because I wanted it to go on forever. Saturday morning I stood at the kitchen window with my heart pounding and my knees shaking. Mother had asked me that morning if I was sure my gingham dress and my pinny were clean, so I was certain my fate was sealed. The big black car drove into the yard, and there he was—this big bear of a man with a brown grain sack in his hand and a fedora on his head. I thought as sure as guns, he's going to put me in that sack. I clung to Mother's dress when she opened the door. How could she be so cheerful? She was going to lose her youngest child.

"Come out to the henhouse," she said. I didn't blame her for not wanting to conduct such a transaction in the house. "Take your pick," she said, and her arm swept over the flock. As he pointed, my brother Everett caught a chicken and put it into the sack, until there were four or five flapping around and cackling inside. It was chickens he was after! Not little seven-year-old girls! Losing my timidity I went up to him and pumped his hand and said how nice it was to meet a banker. He patted my ringlets and took a nickel from his pocket and gave it to me. And then he gave my mother a whole two-dollar bill, which of course went right into the blue sugar bowl.

When I asked her if we owed the banker money, she laughed and said, "No, that debt was paid long ago. He will be buying chickens and eggs from us, and from now on, he will owe me," and she laughed merrily.

Camp Clothes

I no longer remember what kind of a camp it was. Perhaps it was run by the United Church, which always seemed to be way ahead of the Lutherans when it came to programs for the children. It may even have been a camp set up by the Girl Guides in Renfrew. And how Marguerite and I got to be invited also remains a mystery.

All I know is that we had to be driven into Renfrew to meet up with a battered old bus and a dozen or so young girls, none of whom I had ever clapped eyes on before. For the first time in my life I was delighted that Marguerite was along. At least she didn't have an ounce of shyness in her entire body. She was soon bossing everyone around as if she owned the place.

The place was a hall over a store on the main street. We were all crowded into the hall while the old bus spewed out black smoke, which travelled right up to the second floor window of the building, from its tailpipe. Two very stern ladies with long sheets of paper stood at the front of the hall and clapped their hands for order.

They wore navy skirts and white long-sleeved cotton blouses with navy ties around their necks. Marguerite, who never missed a trick, noticed they also had big black whistles on ropes under their collars. Marguerite said she didn't like the look of the whistles. She said this was getting to look more and more like the Northcote school. I was too thrilled about going off to a camp to complain.

The two women were standing in front of a long table and we could see several piles of clothes heaped at one end. One of the women, the one with the pinched lips and the tiny little steel-rimmed glasses, started sorting us into order of size. Then she stood us in front of the appropriate piles of clothing and pointed a long skinny finger in the direction of the table. Marguerite and I were the same size. We looked at the pile of white and navy blue vestments and wondered what we had to do next, since we were both fully clothed, as was every other girl in the room.

The woman with braids wrapped around her head said, "Now take off your clothes and put these on. Then we will all be the same." Obedient as always, I began to unbutton my dress. Marguerite stood like a statue. "Look at this," she hissed. And she held up a huge pair of knickers made of heavy navy blue serge. "I am not going to wear these. They're ugly." One of the women heard the exchange and moved over to our section of the table. She ran a scrawny finger down her sheet of paper. "Marguerite, is it? Well, Marguerite, you *are* going to wear the knickers." And she smiled with tight lips at the defiant youngster. I was already into mine. I looked like a clown, but if this woman said to wear the knickers then that's exactly what I would do.

But she was going to have trouble with Marguerite. I could see it coming. Marguerite squared her shoulders as she always did when she made up her mind that she wasn't going to do something. The woman with the tight lips moved around the table with the knickers under her arm. She had no trouble overpowering Marguerite. She tossed her onto the bench against the wall, sat beside her and moved in front of Marguerite, whose eyes began to bulge as if to say, "I can't believe this is happening to me." The woman leaned over and forced Marguerite's feet into the knicker legs, stuffing her full skirt inside as well. By this time every eye in the room was on them, but it was plain to see Mrs. Steel-Rimmed Glasses had won the round.

We were marched onto the bus in the blinding heat, and the blue serge bloomers stuck to our bodies like sticky flypaper. Marguerite's looked like inflated balloons, with her clothes stuffed inside the legs. I was secretly rejoicing to think that someone had finally won out over the young girl who caused such havoc at the Northcote school, where she always got her own way and, for reasons I was never able to fathom, kept Miss Crosby wrapped around her finger.

We weren't gone a mile outside of Renfrew when Marguerite began complaining about the heat. She fanned herself and said she was dangerously hot, as she called it . . . whatever that meant. The next thing we knew she was having some sort of a seizure, slumped in her seat . . . only I noticed she was careful not to hit her head on the steel arm.

"Take off the knickers, take off the knickers," she was moaning in a faint voice. "I'm going to smother." What the knickers had to do with her breathing was beyond me. But the two women pulled the serge bloomers off and began to fan Marguerite with the pad with all our names on it. Her recovery was almost instantaneous.

The bus started off again, and when the two women were assured Marguerite was not going to expire, they moved to their seats at the front. Marguerite's head was resting on the back of the seat, and in a whisper I could barely hear, she said, "I told you I wouldn't wear those hateful bloomers, and I meant it." Often I wished I could be like Marguerite . . . but alas, I was too meek and mild, and, I have to admit, not nearly as clever. ⸺

The Lawn Bowlers

I used to think Grandfather was the smartest man ever to step foot in Renfrew County. Not only did he drive a rumble seat Ford, but he dressed like a real sport . . . with white polished shoes and grey flannel pants, and a silk scarf in the neck of his shirt, even on the hottest day of the summer.

I loved it when Grandfather visited us on the farm, but I liked it even better on the occasions we visited him in Ottawa. He lived in a yellow brick apartment house on Wellington Street, near the Somerset Street bridge. This put him in close proximity to his work at the Ottawa car barns. He could walk there and be home for lunch any day he chose.

At least once or twice a summer I was allowed to visit my grandparents in Ottawa for a few days. Mother would pack my belongings in a cardboard suitcase, and Grandfather would let me sit in the rumble seat all the way into the city. I was terrified and overjoyed all at the same time. I can remember that trip as giving me the most exciting feeling of anticipation. Occasionally my grandparents would tap the window that separated us, and I would tap back to assure them I was all right and coming along right behind them.

I always had my own room when I visited the grandparents, which was another reason I was overjoyed to be there. At home on the farm I shared the room and the bed with my sister Audrey. Here I had a massive double bed all to myself, with a felt mattress, not feathers like we had at home . . . and I thought my grandparents must be very rich indeed to be able to afford such luxury.

Grandfather always tried to do things with me on those visits. On Saturdays we would go over to Hull for lunch to a little restaurant he was fond of. I can remember they always brought a little plate of cheese pieces before we ordered, and he would let me wrap them in the paper serviette and take them home. I could have iced tea too. I was never allowed that at home, since tea was considered a drink for adults only. But Grandfather would order two large glasses, which I drank with great gusto . . . always afraid that someone would come and take it from me when they found out I was only seven years old.

Grandfather was a great sportsman. He played lacrosse with Newsy Lalonde, who was a cousin, and he golfed as well. But the sport I loved the most, because I was allowed to go and watch him play, was lawn bowling.

I no longer remember where the greens were, but I do remember we had to drive in the car to get there. There were long flat-topped buildings at one end, painted stark white, with green roofs. A row of wide doors opened right out onto the green, and long benches allowed the players to sit and watch the game.

Grandfather knew everyone in the city of Ottawa, I thought at the time. People at the club would come and speak to him, and pat my long red ringlets, and welcome me to the bowling green just as if I were a member.

All the women were dressed in pure white. I remember thinking they looked just like nurses and doctors. The women wore white socks rolled down to their shoes, and the men wore white duck pants and open-necked dress shirts.

I was fascinated, watching them play their game. I had no idea what the object was, or how they kept score, but there would be little bursts of polite applause if someone did something notable. I was aware that Grandfather must have been an especially good bowler, because he got lots of little claps. When that happened, I too clapped from my seat in front of the clubhouse.

The women brought thermoses of lemonade and tin boxes of homemade cookies to eat between games. Many of them had bright parasols, which they held over their heads when they weren't bowling. I thought the bowlers were the most elegant group of people all gathered in one place that I had ever seen . . . even more elegant than the ladies of Northcote who went to the strawberry social at the Lutheran Church, and *they* were pretty elegant with their white gloves and big hats.

That bowling green was very far removed from the farm in Renfrew County. And I doubt that Grandfather ever knew what a sheer joy it was for me to go with him and watch him play. Many times I have driven the streets of Ottawa West looking for that club with its green rolling lawns and sparkling white clubhouse, but try as I might I have never been able to find the Bowling Club. It too, I suppose, like so many memories of that era, has gone. And gone too, I suppose, are most of those elegant ladies and gentlemen who thrilled the heart of a young farm girl of the 1930s.

Aunt Lizzie's Tight Squeeze

I thought Aunt Lizzie was the smartest looking passenger to ever step onto the platform at the Renfrew Station. Apart from her beautiful attire, which always included pure white and bright red, there was that tall slim figure and the carriage of a queen.

She was my father's older sister, and he tolerated her, but that was about all. Father said she turned the homestead upside down every time she came, and as far as he was concerned she could stay in the West, where she belonged.

But every summer she travelled to Renfrew County on her husband's free pass, and for two weeks occupied the boy's back bedroom which she claimed was hers when she was a little girl. Every time she made that remark Father could be heard muttering under his breath, "And that wasn't yesterday." When he really wanted to annoy Aunt Lizzie, all he had to do was say she had put on a bit of beef since her last visit. She vowed she hadn't gained an ounce.

Whereas my mother wore Dan River housedresses in the daytime on the farm, Aunt Lizzie dressed to the nines. She brought enough clothes to dress half the county, and this fact alone thrilled me, because I never knew what she would have on when she descended the stairs for breakfast in the morning.

We always had a Saturday night house party when Aunt Lizzie was visiting from Regina, on her request. She said it was an opportunity to visit with all her old friends. Father said it was an opportunity to put on the dog and generally make a show of how well off she was now that she had left Renfrew County.

I thought Aunt Lizzie had a wonderful figure. She was as tall as my mother, with a figure like an hourglass. I wanted to grow up to look just like her. When I told Father that, he said I could look like that right now if I wanted; all I had to do was seek the help of a few artificial aids . . . whatever that meant.

That year the Saturday night house party was planned for the weekend just before Aunt Lizzie was to go home. She said she wanted to dress with particular care, because an old beau she had gone with years before was coming, with his backwoods wife, as Aunt Lizzie called her.

Our whole family was ready. We were in our next-to-Sunday best, and the big pot of green tea was boiling on the back of the stove. Then we heard Aunt Lizzie roar from the bedroom. Mother and I took the stairs two at a time. Father never took his eyes off the *Ottawa Farm Journal*. There was Aunt Lizzie, ramrod straight, half-dressed, with something around her middle that had more strings and laces than I had ever seen in my life. She was hanging onto the bedpost for dear life, and if the red face was any indication, she was choking to death.

She asked Mother to pull the laces even tighter. I sat on the bed and looked her over from head to toe. I had never seen one of those contraptions before in my life. And I couldn't imagine why anyone would wear one. It looked like sheer torture. "Tighter, Mabel," Aunt Lizzie ordered. "If I pull it any tighter, Lizzie, your back will meet your front," Mother replied. The laces were wrapped around Aunt Lizzie's waist and tied at the back, and big wads of cotton that were sitting on the washstand were being stuffed into her bosom. It sure was a strange sight.

Finally the ordeal was over. Mother helped her slip her pure white silk dress over her head, and the apparition underneath didn't show at all. Aunt Lizzie looked ten pounds lighter, and I was happy to see her face had returned to its normal colour. Mother and I were shooshed from the room so that Aunt Lizzie could apply her make-up in privacy.

On the way downstairs, I asked Mother if I could be the one to tell the family about what Aunt Lizzie had to wear . . . I was sure it was something her doctor had ordered for a bad back. Mother said it was best not to mention the corset at all . . . that the secret would just be between the three of us. I said I thought Father would like to know how much pain his sister was in. Mother said she was sure he would, but it would just add fuel to an already roaring fire . . . whatever that meant.

Charlie and the Buttons

Although Arnprior was considered a healthy drive from Northcote, we visited my father's relatives there frequently. It would take us about two hours in the old Model T. Most of the roads were washboard, and we shook and rattled and fixed flat tires all the way there. But those hindrances never stopped us. Visiting the Prenslers and the Wagonblass aunts and uncles was a treat.

My father's elderly Aunt Roseanne was especially dear to me. She lived in a yellow frame house close to the Kenwood Mill, and her yard was full of vegetables and flowers. When I was just a little girl, perhaps six or seven, Aunt Roseanne was already a very old lady. Aunt Nellie, her married daughter, who was my father's age, lived one street over.

In Aunt Roseanne's house lived a son. Charlie was considered very strange. He had been badly hurt as a baby when the homestead was being built, and had never learned to speak. Instead he talked in grunts and used hand gestures which I always considered menacing. Charlie was the only thing I didn't like about going to Aunt Roseanne's.

The things I liked best were her gooseberry jam made from fruit right out of her own backyard, and her huge wicker button box. Aunt Roseanne was always sewing or embroidering or knitting when we visited her in Arnprior. Her gnarled hands were never idle.

Sometimes Mother would drop me off at Aunt Roseanne's, and she'd go to visit Aunt Nellie, or walk through the stores on the main street. On those occasions I stayed very close to the elderly lady, because I was terrified of Charlie. She sensed I was nervous too, because she would send him into the garden to pick beans. One day she made him scrub the veranda on his hands and knees. It looked perfectly clean to me, as did everything else in Aunt Roseanne's house. But it kept Charlie occupied.

One day late in the summer, I had been dropped off at the yellow frame house. Aunt Roseanne was sitting on a big fanback wooden lawn chair in the yard, and when I went up to her to be hugged in greeting, she immediately sent Charlie into the house for the cookie jar.

He came out with her wicker button box. He shuffled right over to me and thrust it in my face. He had a large white flourbag tea cloth as well, and he spead it out on the grass beside me. I had no idea what I was supposed to do. I looked up at Aunt Roseanne for direction. She was intent on her sewing and offered me no help.

Charlie shuffled from one foot to the other. I stared at the cloth and the button box. Finally he dropped to his knees beside me, giving me a start. Then he dumped the button box out on the tea cloth. There were hundreds and hundreds of buttons . . . all shapes and sizes and colours. I had never seen so many buttons in my life. Charlie ran his hands over them, spreading them out before me.

He sat back on his haunches waiting for me to make the next move. His cloudy eyes never left my face, and I could feel the perspiration running down my back. What did he want me to do? I again looked over to Aunt Roseanne. She was humming softly and all I could hear was the clicking of her scissors as she cut away a hem on an old coat.

Charlie reached into his pocket and brought out a handful of short pieces of string. They lay like spaghetti on the cloth. Then he started matching the buttons, all into little piles. Big black coat buttons in one heap, white shirt buttons in another. He gestured awkwardly to the piles. I ran my hands over the buttons spread out on the ground and began finding mates too. I made a little pile of green buttons with white centres. There were about six big red buttons like those on Mother's Dan River cotton housedress. Charlie would add to mine, and I to his.

When we had about ten piles, Charlie took one of the short pieces of string, threaded it through the button holes of each set, and tied them firmly together. I did the same thing. Soon we had dozens of bundles of buttons, all tied together. Occasionally Charlie would raise his eyes and say something I could not understand. I would nod as if I knew exactly what he was trying to tell me. I was no longer afraid of him. Our hands would touch as we sorted through the mounds of buttons. Like two little children we played together for hours with his mother's button box. Never again was I afraid to visit Aunt Roseanne's house in Arnprior. This grown man with the mind of a little child, and the young girl from a backwoods farm in Renfrew County, had found a common ground . . . an old wicker button box and a handful of pieces of string.

A New Car?

The morning broke hot and humid like every day before it over the past few weeks. When the chores were done Father headed for the drive shed. The three brothers were close behind. It took the four of them to push the old Model T out into the yard. Father lifted the tin hoods that concealed the motor and put his head inside as far as it would go. On the other side of the car, the three brothers did likewise.

Everett was told to get behind the wheel and Father went around to the front with the crank. As always, I stood well back, partly because I was scared to death the thing would kick and Father's arm would fly off into a nearby tree. Or at the very least, he would erupt into a fit of rage and start cussing in German, which always brought Mother charging from the summer kitchen.

Whichever course trying to start the car took, it was not a pleasant experience. That morning proved to be no different. Father cranked and cranked. Emerson ran to get some water from the rain barrel to pour into the hole in the radiator. And then, just as everyone was about to give up, the old Ford coughed and sputtered and flew into action. There it sat on its four spindly tires, throbbing like a horse with the heaves. Father yelled over the din that he was going to let it run a spell, and he yanked down the gas lever under the steering wheel. Just then steam started to spout out the radiator, and it hissed like a snake and blew the cap right back into the drive shed. Father ran to shut off the motor, and the thing came to a grinding halt, shuddered, and died. Father pitched his straw hat to the ground and jumped up and down on it. "It's got to go. That's all there is to it. It's got to go!" And he stormed into the house to discuss the matter with Mother.

Not wanting to miss the action, we children crowded around the kitchen table to hear Father's pitch. Thacker's garage in Renfrew had advertised a second-hand car in last week's *Mercury*, and he would probably give him a few dollars for the old Model T, and the time had come, the Ford had had its day. Our heads moved between Father and Mother and our excitement grew as Mother, to our surprise, agreed with everything Father was saying. "There is only one problem, Albert," she said. "Where is the money going to come from to pay the difference?" Father didn't say a word. There was silence for the longest time.

Then Mother said she was quite sure she could round up a few more customers for sticky buns in Renfrew, and the hens had been laying awfully well, and maybe another couple pounds of butter a week would bring in a bit of money. "Why don't you go and see Mr. Thacker?" We all jumped up and down and asked to go too. Mother said we couldn't take a chance on getting into Renfrew in the Model T, and the last thing Father needed was five children stranded on the side of the road twelve miles from home. So Father and the brothers once again nursed the old car into action and we watched as it headed out the lane, slowly and not so surely, for the long drive into town.

We could hardly stand the wait for Father's return. Emerson said he was sure the car would be grey . . . always wanted a grey car, he mused, with his eyes heavenward. Everett said a sedan would be nice. Audrey said she didn't care what it loked like as long as it would go more than a mile without a flat tire.

All afternoon we waited for the new car to come into view. And then we saw, first, the dust from the long lane, and finally, the car as it wheeled into the barnyard. But it wasn't a sedan . . . it wasn't grey . . . it was the same old Model T Father had left in. It came limping towards the house, the motor thumping and the steam spewing out of the hood. Father drove it right into the drive shed. We knew it would be just a matter of time before we heard why the big trade hadn't taken place.

Chores were done, the reservoir filled, and the kitchen redded up after supper. Mother finally brought up the subject. "Well, let's put it this way, Mabel," Father said from his spot in the rocking chair by the table. "If those chickens each laid ten eggs a day, everyone in Renfrew bought at least two dozen sticky buns a week, and we could draw enough cream from the cows to make about twenty-five pounds of butter every Saturday, we might have enough money to trade." He snapped open the *Renfrew Mercury*. We all knew the subject was closed. ━

New-Fangled Miracles

I think now that doing the weekly washing was harder on my Mother in the summertime than it was in the winter. Even though on the most beastly of cold days the laundry had to be hung out on the line, doing the wash in a hot summer kitchen was worse. I can still see my mother with the perspiration running down her face, pounding the clothes in the copper tub with a wash pole and rubbing the heavily soiled things on the tin washboard. And all the time more water would be heating on the roaring cookstove ready for the next tub.

Father knew what a chore it was too. Before he would go to the barns in the morning, he would bail out the reservoir for Mother and pour it into the copper tub, all the while saying what a hard job it was doing the weekly washing. Then he would turn to my sister Audrey and me and say, "Now, you girls help your mother, you hear?"

And then one day—a Monday it was too—Father left the barnyard early in the morning after helping Mother fill the tub. He said he was going into town to fetch some binder twine. "I'll be back by dinner," he said, meaning, of course, the mid-day meal.

It was an especially hot day, and Mother, who usually sang or whistled all the time she worked, was silent. She was intent on finishing the job before the sun was overhead and beating down on the summer kitchen roof.

Every so often she would straighten up and rub the small of her back and push the hair back from her face. I wanted so badly to make her workload easier, but only one pair of hands would fit in the washtub . . . and besides, there was only one washboard.

Audrey and I carried the basket of clothes outside and hung

them on the line; when it was full, we draped them over the fence; and finally, we laid the last few pieces out on the grass. The job was done for another week. Mother washed her face in cold well water, and collapsed on the couch in the parlour to sit a spell and cool off.

We heard Father drive into the yard with the wagon and heard him holler for the brothers to come and help him. Couldn't imagine why he needed anyone to help unload binder twine. The summer kitchen door opened with a bang, and we heard Father and the boys dragging something across the floor. Mother rose from the couch and Audrey and I followed her.

There, sitting in the corner of the room, was a brand new washing machine. We had no electricity, of course, so it was completely hand operated. It had a wooden tub and a long arm at the side which operated the washer. And attached to the top was a hand-worked ringer with a crank affair to turn it.

Mother stood and looked at it for a long time and then she went to it and rubbed her hands all over the smooth wood. I hugged the tub part, and Emerson was already turning the wringer. Mother didn't even ask Father how much it cost, or where the money came from.

I wondered if we could keep it. Maybe he had just borrowed it. But no, Father assured me it was there to stay.

Mother went over to the Findlay Oval and lifted the reservoir lid. The water Audrey had replaced was already steaming. I knew exactly what she was thinking.

She sent Everett for the small pail we used for bailing out the reservoir and Earl was asked to sliver some homemade lye soap into the new tub. Audrey was sent upstairs to strip a bed . . . any bed, she was told. I reminded Mother the beds had just been changed. "Nothing like fresh sheets on a hot summer day," Mother said.

Soon the tub was full of water and clean bed sheets. We all took turns pumping the side handle, but when it came time to wring the clothes Mother said it was too dangerous for anyone but her to use the hand-operated wringer. We watched the sheets being fed into this miracle piece of machinery, and I couldn't believe my eyes. A flat piece of shiny tin poured the water back into the tub as neat as you please as the sheets were wrung out. There was no doubt about it—this new-fangled washing machine was going to change our lives.

And it did. No more Monday mornings dreaded. I knew there were some neighbours who had generators to run their washing machines. And some, a very few, had electricity. But there were others who only had what we had before this wonderful invention arrived. Yes, the hand washer was indeed a step up for us.

⇜ Church Games ⇝

It was the custom back in the 1930s at our little country church to hold a sort of celebration at the end of the summer. It meant simply that the hot sticky weather was over, school had started, and once again the pews were full at the Lutheran Church. This last fact was reason enough to hold a celebration, according to our minister, who was a whale of a man who lived in a black suit, shiny from wear.

Once church service was over, the day was given over to frivolity. There were games for the children, three-legged races, an ample lunch served by the ladies of the church, and a rousing hymn sing at the end of the festivities to signify the event had come to a close. Mother considered this last event a clever move, since she maintained the farmers in Renfrew County never knew enough to go home, and without the hymn sing, everyone would probably still be there at sun-up.

There were little handmade ribbons for the winners of the events, highly coveted, and the winners wore them pinned to their sweaters and jackets long into the fall. So there was a real feeling of competitiveness during most of the afternoon. As it happened, my cousin Ronny, visiting for the summer, was still with us into the early fall that year. Even though he was much younger than Cecil, the two had formed a friendship. That wasn't at all unusual, because both boys were well known for their pranks, and their antics drew them together like magnets.

That day there were to be dog races. This usually meant two children worked together. One held the dog while the other went to the other end of the churchyard and enticed it any way he could to run as fast as possible to the finishing line. Cecil had an old cull of a dog that was a sight to behold. It had two different coloured eyes, and one and a half ears. It had lost the other half in a scrap with a gobbler. Its hind legs seemed to be longer than its front ones, which Emerson said was an impossibility . . . but I know for a fact there was something misshapen about the whole dog.

At any rate, the dog was entered in the races. Ronny and Cecil had been working with him for days. It was decided to separate the dogs well in the line-up because once two of them had gotten into an awful scrap and the whole event was almost cancelled. So there was Ronny at the finish line, and Cecil way across the churchyard with the dog. The minister was standing at the centre with a cap gun.

It went off with a bang, and the dogs went everywhere but towards the finish line. Somebody yelled, "False start," and the dogs were hauled back to the starting position. Cecil said he thought they would run better if they were separated even further. Everyone thought this made perfect sense. By now the line-up of dogs was stretched right across the churchyard, with Cecil farthest away.

The minister closed his eyes and pointed the cap gun heavenward. Another explosion rocked the air.

Cecil's dog let out a yelp that could be heard in Admaston, and it took off like a cannon. Its haunches were right to the ground, but it was paying no attention to Ronny, who was screaming at it to go towards him. It circled the yard about fifty times, yelping all the way. Most of the other dogs stopped a few feet from the starting line, and a few of them wandered off to a tree or towards the lunch table to see if they could pick up a few scraps. Cecil's dog was finally cornered by Ronny, and even though it came nowhere near the finish line, was declared the winner for sheer effort.

I saw Cecil and Ronny walking towards the back of our old car and they looked pretty sheepish to me. I saw them throw something into the long grass and I waited until I got the chance to go and retrieve whatever it was. All I could find was an empty turpentine bottle, but it certainly looked as if it had been used recently. I had no idea what connection it had with the dog races, but I was reasonably sure there *was* a connection.

The two young villains were crouched at the back end of the car and their whispers carried right to where I was standing. Ronny said Cecil had probably maimed the dog for life. Cecil said not to be so crazy, his father used turpentine to rub the horses' legs with all the time. Ronny reminded Cecil it wasn't the dog's legs which had gotten the treatment. Cecil said a good swim in the Bonnechere would cure it. I had no idea what they were talking about. But the dog had finally ended its fit of running and was lying on the grass by the gate exhausted.

The two boys looked like model citizens as the minister called out their names as the winners of the dog race. They claimed their ribbons and allowed the minister to pin them to their shirts.

"Well done, my lads," said the reverend gentleman. They beamed up into his face like perfect angels, and smoothed out the curled-up edges of their ribbons. I was convinced more than ever that the turpentine bottle had more than a little to do with winning the race. ➤

Depression Hospitality

I never thought we were poor when we lived through those Depression years on the farm in the 1930s. Oh, Mother often referred to the lack of money, and Father peppered his speeches on thrift with phrases like, "don't you know there is a Depression on?" as if it were something we could reach out and touch. We certainly didn't have too many frills, but I never once thought of us as being desperately poor. It was only years later that I realized how destitute we were.

On the other hand, I thought our relatives from Ottawa were poor. They had to buy their tomatoes, and their milk. And a man delivered their blocks of ice for the ice box and charged them fifty cents a week! Our blocks were chopped out of the Bonnechere River, and whenever we needed a tomato we went to the garden, and we had more milk than we knew what to do with.

Another reason I always thought my Ottawa relatives were poor was that Father said they came out to the farm when they were hungry, which was pretty often. They never missed an opportunity to come out for a good meal, which my mother was most adept at pulling together from the barrels of meat in the summer kitchen and the produce we grew in our garden. Every fall we could count on a few carloads pouring into our yard after church to have what they called a good stickin'-to-the-ribs kind of dinner. They came in an assortment of old battered cars, and by the time we got home from church several aunts and uncles and cousins would have already arrived. Some of them would be waiting on the back stoop and others would be inside the old log house where the doors were never locked.

Mother wasn't surprised that relatives poured out of the city to visit us, and she was always prepared for a gang at the Sunday table.

If the number grew beyond what she was ready for, she simply sent Everett out to the chicken coop for an extra bird for the pot!

I realize now that is probably why we usually had a huge white enamelled pot of chicken and dumplings on the stove on Sunday. You could add to it as the crowd increased. The chicken would have been cut into pieces and put on the back of the stove in the morning to simmer gently with onions until we got home from church.

We children liked it when these crowds of relatives poured into the farm. My cousins loved the hay mow. They had nothing to compare with it in the city of Ottawa. My brothers thought they were all sissies, and spent a lot of their visit testing their nerves. They would let the old ram out of the pen, or the gobbler, which could always be trusted to make a lunge for whatever or whomever was in its way. The boys often ended up rolling on the floor of the barn in a roary-eyed fight. And when the city cousins emerged from the tangle, there wasn't one iota of resemblance to the immaculate boys who had stepped out of the cars a few hours before.

My sister Audrey and I and our girl cousins wouldn't indulge in such antics, but rather spent the time either playing with our dolls in an upstairs bedroom, or listening to my cousins boast about all the boys they knew at the city schools. Evelyn wore nail polish, which Audrey and I considered the height of fashion. And she had cuban-heeled shoes and a permanent in her hair. We thought she was extremely elegant for a fifteen-year-old.

When it was time to gather around the old kitchen table, which had been extended to accommodate as many as possible, we always found there wasn't a spot for the children. So Father would bring in an old pine door from the drive shed, and put it across two saw horses in the parlour, and we children ate there. We loved the segregation from the adults. The talk was of street cars and swimming in a pool called Plant's Bath, and sandwiches with uncles at Bowles Lunch in Ottawa. We loved to hear them talk of these places that we knew we would never be part of. The fight in the barn would soon be forgotten.

We children would run into the kitchen to have our plates replenished from heaping bowls on the kitchen table. I would always stop a minute to watch Uncle Johnny DeGray eat. He was a tall man, well over six feet, with a shiny bald head and a ring of white hair over his ears. He had enormous gnarled hands, which my mother said got that way from driving a big steam roller on Ottawa's streets, which was his job. And he ate as if it was going to be his last meal on earth. I marvelled then, and to this day, at the amount of food he could pack away.

When the meal was over, the men would retire to the drive shed to smoke their pipes or cigars, and the women would wash the dishes on the kitchen table. And always Mother would fill a big sealer jar with leftover chicken and dumplings for Uncle Johnny to take back to Ottawa. No one left the yard without cabbages, potatoes, and sand-caked carrots from the root cellar.

It was when they were driving out of the yard that Father inevitably said, "Well, there they go, with a good meal in their bellies and the car full of food." Mother would reach over and pat his hand and say, "There, there, Albert. Aren't we lucky to have it to give?" It was then the Depression seemed a great distance away from that old log house in Renfrew County. —

The Lunch Box

"I hate green," Cecil said through clenched teeth and with his eyes crossed. He righted them long enough to glare at Marguerite, who was the object of his comment. Or, rather, her lunch box was. It was brand spanking new and bright green, with a little girl dressed in red and a skipping rope painted on the side. It was a little tin box with handles, and I was so envious I didn't know how I was going to make it to recess without killing Marguerite on that first day of school.

She was the only one in the entire school who wouldn't have to carry her lunch in her book bag, wrapped in brown bread paper, or simply thrust into a paper bag along with notebooks and pencils. The rest of us removed our lunches from our book bags and put them on the table at the back of the room as we always did. There, standing in the midst of the plainly wrapped lunches, was Marguerite's tin box, as conspicuous as a heifer on a highway.

"Boy, does she think she's somebody," Cecil tossed over his shoulder just as Miss Crosby ordered us to take our assigned seats. Cecil dropped into the first desk at the back of the school, but with his reputation, we knew he wouldn't be there long. Recess came and went, and Marguerite adjusted her green lunch box so that it was more prominently placed at the front of the table.

When the big CPR clock struck twelve noon, after a nod from Miss Crosby, we lined up to wash our hands in the basin at the back door. I was reluctant to claim my lunch bag, knowing full well Marguerite would have inside that green pail things like store-bought bread, cold meat from Briscoe's, and maybe even a piece of fresh fruit from Renfrew. She tossed her artificial curls in my direction, and as she retrieved her elegant green lunch box, said she thought taking a lunch in a brown paper bag was just about the most uncivilized act she could think of.

We girls from the Northcote school always ate our lunches together, under the big maple tree at the side of the gate. We sat on the grass and watched the boys at the other end of the yard.

Everyone except Marguerite had unwrapped her sandwiches—mostly jelly they were—and we were taking turns drinking well water out of the one chipped porcelain cup which hung at the pump. Marguerite had waited to open her lunch pail so that we would all have the full benefit of the exercise. "I have a thermos of milk. It fits on a little wire holder inside my brand new lunch box," she said. "I hate milk," I said.

She made a great to-do of opening the box, fully aware that the eyes of nine girls from the Northcote school were upon her. There was a gasp, and her chubby hand flew to her mouth. She didn't even wait to close the lid, but struggled to her feet and headed for the school door, yelling "Miss Crosby!" at the top of her lungs. Beatrice was the first to grab the lunch box. All that was in it was the crust of a sandwich with the whole inside eaten out, and about fifty grasshoppers. The thermos cork and the screw-on cup proved that the milk had either been poured out or consumed. The grasshoppers were jumping every which way, and one had even jumped inside the thermos. Every eye in the group sought out Cecil at the other side of the schoolyard. He looked like a choir boy with his lunch spread out before him on the grass.

When Miss Crosby came out she was pressing her temples with the tips of her fingers, and I knew she was wondering if this was going to be another one of those years.

Cecil flatly denied having anything to do with the deed, and no one else would own up to it either. Miss Crosby questioned each one of us in turn while Marguerite stood behind her skirt for protection and looked at her shiny new green lunch box still sitting under the maple tree. When there was no apology forthcoming, Miss Crosby said the whole school would miss afternoon recess. No one seemed to care. On the way back into the school Cecil could be heard asking Edward if he would help him round up a garter snake the next morning. "I think I know where I could use one," he said with his eyes slit in Marguerite's direction.

We saw Marguerite pale and clutch the lunch box to her chest. She left the schoolyard at four o'clock on a dead run and the last we saw of her on that first day of school was hair flying and patent leather shoes just barely touching the ground. It was also the last we ever saw of the green lunch box.

New Shoes

I was sick and tired of wearing boy's brogues to school. But until I was about seven years old that's all that ever touched my feet. The brothers grew at such a rate that they rarely wore out their footwear, even after it was handed down from Everett to Emerson and finally to Earl. And so it was always my lot in life to eventually be given the hateful brown laced-up shoes when they no longer fit the boys. "Still plenty of good wear in those," Mother would say, handing them over to me and expecting me to be overjoyed and grateful. I admit they often looked brand new, because they were only worn on Sunday or for going into town. The boys wore gum rubbers the rest of the time.

My sister Audrey was allowed to wear shoes that came right out of the shoe store in Renfrew. She was older, my mother said. And I wondered when I would reach the magical age when I too would be too old to wear my brothers' brogues.

That day came much sooner than I expected, and through a strange turn of events. And it all had to do with bad Marguerite, Marguerite of the black patent leather Mary Jane shoes. No brogues for her. And I doubt she ever wore a hand-me-down in her entire life. Even though Marguerite and I were such arch-enemies, our mothers were friends, a fact which gave me no comfort whatsoever.

One day Marguerite's mother was at our house when I got home after school. She and Mother were having a cup of tea in the parlour . . . no entertaining in the kitchen for the likes of her. Like mother, like daughter, I thought. She looked right down at my brown laced-up boy's brogues. "Bad for a girl's feet," she said. "Much too wide . . . brogues are made for boys. I have never let

Marguerite wear hand-me-down shoes." I waited for Mother to defend the shoes, but she said nothing. "I think Marguerite is much bigger than Mary and she has a pair of lovely shoes she has grown out of. Perhaps I could bring them over."

And that's when Mother's mixture of Irish temper and French pride took over. She said she needn't bother. In fact, Mother went on, she planned on going into Renfrew that Saturday for the express purpose of getting Mary a new pair of girl's shoes. Well, that was sure news to me. I noticed Mother didn't say anything about black patent leather Mary Janes. But I vowed I wouldn't care . . . they could be made of duck feathers for all of me . . . as long as they looked like girl's shoes.

Well, that Saturday, as good as her word, Mother went into town loaded down with double the amount of fresh sticky buns, three days' worth of eggs and fresh butter, as well as our weekly offering of drawn and dressed chickens. And we came home with a pair of soft leather girl's shoes, the likes of which I had never seen before. They had buckles . . . no laces, and a design on the front. I though they had Marguerite's Mary Janes beat by a country mile.

Before I went to school that Monday morning, Mother put newspaper inside my galoshes to protect my brand new shoes, and I went off down the Northcote side road crunching like I was walking in two paper bags. But I didn't care a hoot.

When I sat in my desk, I still wasn't sure everyone had seen the new shoes. And at that time in my life, that was very important to me. So instead of sitting with my feet under my desk, I stuck them straight out in the aisle. Marguerite would have to be blind not to notice.

But alas, it was Miss Crosby who put an end to my vanity. "Feet flat on the floor, and under the desk," she said when she came down the aisle. But she said it so low that only I could hear. And she patted my shoulder and in a much louder voice said, "lovely shoes, Mary." I tucked my feet under where they belonged, but that day was pretty well spent looking down to make sure the shoes were still there and that I hadn't imagined the whole affair. I never once thought of how hard Mother had to work to buy them. But today I like to think she got as much satisfaction out of the new store-bought girl's shoes as I did.

Waste Not, Want Not

We passed the big apple tree every day of our lives going to and coming from the Northcote school. It didn't belong to anyone. It grew right on the side of the road, a big sprawling tree which bore wonderful bright red apples. We sometimes stopped and picked one off the limbs and munched it on the way home from school. But we never thought of them as much of a treat, as we had a good-sized orchard in our own back yard, and more than enough apples to satisfy our cravings.

There must have been eight or ten of us walking the Northcote side road coming home from school that day. Cecil, who could think up more mischief to get into than an entire school full of kids put together, said it had sure been a quiet day. We were just coming to the apple tree and Cecil stopped dead in his tracks and looked it up and down as if he had never laid eyes on it before in his life.

He slid down into the ditch and yanked an apple off the branch over his head. He tossed it in the direction of Emerson, who caught it on the first try. Cecil grabbed another one and burned it by Everett.

From there, the gang of us divided into two sides, and Cecil, as was his custom, took complete charge. He sent half of us on one side of the rail fence and the rest stood in the ditch. And soon there was a battle royal going on. Apples were flying everywhere. We younger girls were sure we were going to be maimed for life, but amazingly enough few apples connected with anyone. Cecil said the object was to see how many apples we could throw against each other's team. And then he said when we were tired of the game, we could count the number of apples on the ground to see which team would win.

Well, let me tell you, those apples flew across that fence like bullets. And soon the only apples left on the tree were those near the top which no one could reach.

Cecil said he was tired of the game, and he and the Thom boys headed off down the Northcote side road. It was Audrey who first heard the car coming over the hill. I was delighted to see it was Mother coming home from town . . . now we would have a ride the rest of the way home.

The dirt flew in every direction as Mother put the brake pedal to the floor. It didn't take someone with a university education to see what we were up to. The ground was full of apples on both sides of the fence, and I wasted no time in telling Mother about the wonderful game we had all played together.

Mother didn't seem to be nearly as excited as I thought she would be. She climbed out of the car and surveyed the scene. She stooped and picked up an apple and bit into it. "Good apples," she declared.

Then her expression changed. It was as if someone had pulled a roller blind down over her face and let it roll up to show an entirely different person.

"Waste. That's what it is. Plain and simple waste. And sinful, too. Don't you know there is a Depression on? Don't you know there are people starving in the cities right in this very country?"

For the life of me I couldn't imagine what an apple fight had to do with the Depression, but I soon found out.

"Well, I'll tell you what you are going to do," she said. And there was an edge to her voice which told us outright that she wasn't a bit pleased. "You are going to stay right here and pick up all those apples and load them into the back seat of the car." No one had the audacity to tell Mother it was starting to get dark. And instead of helping us, she climbed back behind the wheel of the Model T and glared out at the lot of us, frantically picking up apples and tossing them into the car.

That wasn't the end of it, either. Long into the evening, back home, Audrey and I peeled apples, the brothers washed them, and we wrapped the best in pieces of newspaper to store for later use. Mother never lifted a finger to help us. But more than once she told us the value of thrift and the evils of waste. When we finally finished the last apple, Mother did as she always did under like circumstances. "Now, did you learn anything?" In unison we all said, "Yes, Mother."

Emerson added under his breath, "Yeah, I learned something all right—if you're going to have an apple fight, make sure it isn't in plain view of your mother." And I could hear him plotting with Everett to take a round out of Cecil the next day at the Northcote school. —

Fear in the Privy

My brother Emerson knew I was terrified of going to the privy at night, especially in the fall of the year, when it was cold into the bargain. Usually my sister Audrey could be persuaded to accompany me on the trip, but sometimes she was busy with something else, and I was left to my own devices . . . to shudder and shake for the few hundred feet between the house and the little grey board structure that served as our bathroom.

Emerson didn't help matters one little bit. He would stand in the woodshed, making the most frightening sounds and opening and closing a squeaky door, a noise that sent chills right through me.

My brothers were quite used to going out to the privy without benefit of flashlight, but I always took a lantern. It offered little light, but I felt more secure carrying it with me. And if all else failed, I would drag our old collie dog out with me, and make him stay outside the door to wait for me. Then I would tear back into the house, never daring to look back in case some evil spirit lay in hiding in the many bushes that surrounded our old log home.

I remember one night in particular. It was as dark as pitch. A rainstorm with strong winds had enveloped the farmhouse all day and into the late evening. To me there was nothing more frightening than going outside to the privy when it was windy and raining, and I sat at the kitchen table putting off the inevitable until I could wait no longer. All evening my brother Emerson had taunted me, saying he could hear something in the woodshed, a lean-to I was forced to walk through on the way to the outside bathroom. Once or twice he went out himself, and each time he said he was sure there was a wild animal circling the privy. All furry and black it was too, he said.

Bedtime was nearing. I could put off going outside no longer. I took a lantern down off the hook at the back door, and watched the tiny flame appear, which gave me no comfort at all. If I didn't hurry, I knew there would soon be no use in making the effort to go out. I grabbed a jacket off another hook, and took one last look around the kitchen. Emerson was sitting at the table; his eyes were like slits and he had a look of impending doom about him. I offered him a licorice pipe I had in my washstand drawer if he would come as far as the woodshed with me.

"Not on your life," he said, shuddering for effect. "I've been out there already, and once was enough for me. Watch for that black bobcat out there . . . it looked real mean."

I made a dash through the woodshed and picked my way along the little path that led to the privy. The lantern was no help at all. The wind howled, and the fall rain pelted my face. At last I was at the little house. I held the lantern high inside and could see no sign of a wild animal, so I went in and closed the door securely behind me. Inside I felt a bit more secure, and toyed with the idea of staying there for the night, or at least until someone came looking for me.

Father had made a little wooden box which hung on the side wall. It held the old Eaton's catalogue, which served as toilet paper in those days. I hung the lantern on the corner of the little box, its slivers of light barely showing me where the door was. Finally it was time to make a decision. I was cold and shivery . . . and I reached into the box for a sheet of the old catalogue. My hand closed around a piece of fur and I screamed bloody murder. I grabbed the lantern, and didn't even wait to retrieve my flourbag underwear off the floor.

I covered the trip back to the house in seconds flat. I told everyone within earshot that a wild animal was in the catalogue box in the backhouse. Father said it was impossible. Mother said I imagined it . . . and Emerson, I noticed, was snickering behind his scribbler. To stop my carrying on, Mother said Father would go out with the lantern to take a look. I stood in the doorway of the woodshed and watched Father enter the little wood building. On my instructions he reached into the catalogue box and pulled out the animal. I watched him turn it over in his hand. He came to the shed.

"There's your bobcat." It was his old fur hat, battered but familiar. No one had to ask how it got there. When we got to the kitchen, Emerson was already on his way to bed . . . the picture of guilt.

Aunt Edith's Dog Chrissy

We always thought it was a blessing Aunt Edith didn't have any children. They would have gotten short shrift. All her attention was lavished on her big orange cat and on a dog the size of a minute by the name of Chrissy. The dog came from dubious background, but as far as Aunt Edith was concerned its parentage might as well have been linked to the Royal Family.

She visited the farm regularly, and always brought one of the pets with her. The other stayed behind at her home in Gananoque with Uncle George. When Aunt Edith came for her annual fall visit, she liked to pick apples from our orchard, and go home with a few baskets of potatoes and onions from the garden.

This particular day was bright and crisp, with a real bite in the air. Aunt Edith drove into the yard with Chrissy draped around her neck like a fur collar. When Aunt Edith crawled out of the car, the dog started to act as if she had been mortally wounded, and she snapped at anyone who went near the car door. It was then we saw the little velvet coat the dog was wearing. We had never seen a dog in a coat before. It was brown, almost the same colour as her fur, and it had four little legs sewn onto it to further keep the cold away.

Emerson went hysterical. He seemed to think it was the funniest thing he had ever seen, and his antics brought a frown to Aunt Edith's face. She couldn't bear to think anyone might be making sport of her beloved Chrissy.

The dog wore the coat all day. That night it was removed while she bedded down with Aunt Edith—a practice Mother heartily disapproved of, but could do little about.

Aunt Edith had been with us about three days when Emerson got the brilliant notion that our old barn cat might benefit from

Chrissy's coat on the chilly fall nights. Chrissy wouldn't be wearing it anyway. And besides, Emerson was dying to try the coat on some creature other than Chrissy. It goes without saying that this plan was not discussed with Mother or Aunt Edith. Aunt Edith would have a purple fit if a barn cat came within fifty feet of her beloved Chrissy.

Now, this old barn cat was a mean one. But Emerson was just as fond of it as Aunt Edith was of her dog. Emerson said the old cat was the smartest animal on the farm. I didn't know about that. But I did know that, next to our horse King, it was the meanest. It would stand up to anyone and anything. I had seen it tackle the gobbler, a bird which in itself was a force to be reckoned with. I felt a surge of excitement when Emerson told me about putting old Allie into the dog's coat. Seldom did my brother count me into his plans.

I might have known I had been consulted because Emerson couldn't carry out his plan without me. When Aunt Edith went up to bed, carrying Chrissy under one arm, I always followed her with a glass of cold well water to put beside her night table. I would watch the nightly ritual with fascination. Aunt Edith would turn over the down cover, fluff up one of the pillows, and strip Chrissy of the brown velvet coat. A glance from her would tell me I was excused.

Emerson said it was my job to get the dog coat out of the bedroom. I could see no problem with that, since Aunt Edith always spent a great deal of time settling Chrissy comfortably into the bed, and the coat was always laid out on the chair at the door.

On the night in question, I got my hands on the coat, and headed for the woodshed where Emerson had coaxed Allie. The cat wasn't at all pleased with the confined space, and was hissing and clawing at the air, the hair on his back standing up like a wire brush. Emerson was having no luck subduing the ugly cat, and I kept my distance, tossing the coat at the two of them. It was a real test of Emerson's endurance, but he managed to get the velvet dog coat on the big ugly cat. It fit him like the peel on an orange. He started clawing at it, broke free of Emerson, and started running in frantic circles around the woodshed.

Unfortunately, Father opened the door just then to bring in an armful of wood, and Allie cleared the doorway and Father's frame in one leap, escaping into the night. We grabbed the lantern and headed for the barn, which is where we assumed the cat would head. There was no sign of him anywhere.

We finally had to call it quits at bedtime. I had no idea what we were going to tell Aunt Edith in the morning.

She searched frantically for the missing coat all day. We said nothing.

In the afternoon, when Father was bringing in the cows, Allie appeared, coming in from the back fields. Parts of the coat were still on him. The legs were missing, the opening was upside down, and whatever was left of the coat was covered with mud.

There was no need to tell Aunt Edith what had happened. All that remained was for two children to run for cover.

The Summer Kitchen

Mother said she wouldn't have made an issue over the summer kitchen if the old log house had been larger. As it was we had one big room which served as a kitchen and dining room, a small bedroom, and a smaller parlour on the bottom floor. Mother said she sure could make use of the summer kitchen all year round. Every spring, the big old Findlay Oval was lugged out to the summer kitchen and then in the late fall it was hauled back into the house.

That year, when we were all enjoying one of the longest Indian summers on record, Mother announced that she thought we should try to keep the summer kitchen open over the winter. She said the heat of the Findlay Oval would just about blast you out of the house on the coldest day, and she saw no reason why it couldn't do the same job in the summer kitchen. Father tried to remind her that there was nothing but boards for walls in the lean-to, the windows wouldn't close tightly, and you could run a two-by-four under the bottom of the door.

Mother called those minor adjustments that would have to be dealt with, and announced that the Findlay Oval was going to stay exactly where it had been since early April. Father as usual decided the best thing to do in such a situation was to let Mother learn the hard way, and the discussion was closed.

The brothers were delighted they wouldn't have to haul the big stove back into the house. It usually took the better part of a Saturday, by the time the pipes were taken down, painted and put back up in the house, and then the big stove had to be hauled inside on logs and planks. Emerson said the day could be better spent hunting rabbits.

Mother set about getting the summer kitchen ready for the onslaught of the severe winters Renfrew County was famous for. She nailed a rolled-up rug to the bottom of the door, and said she would defy the wind to penetrate it. She stuffed the crooked window frames with old wool socks, and ran newspapers in every crack in the walls she could find. Then she revved up the old Findlay Oval and we children admitted that the summer kitchen was just about as hot as the inside of our old log house on the coldest Ottawa Valley winter day. Mother was beaming over her success and raving about how nice it would be to have more room in the main part of our living quarters. Father could be heard muttering under his breath in German, which meant to all of us that he had no patience for anyone who had so little respect for Renfrew County winters.

Indian summer continued on for a time, with each day getting just a little bit colder, but Mother kept the Findlay Oval jumping and the house was as cozy as could be. It cooled off at night, however, since the pipes no longer snaked through the upstairs hall. Mother said we'd get used to it, and besides, the heat would soon waft in from the summer kitchen. That comment earned her a raised eyebrow and a snort from Father.

By the middle of December the cold weather got down to serious business. The snow came one night out of nowhere, and you could see your breath in the bedrooms upstairs. No one wanted to get out of bed. The wind was howling and the window panes were covered with snow and frost. The ankles of our long underwear which we had washed out the night before were frozen solid at the foot of our beds.

Audrey suggested we grab our clothes and make a beeline for the summer kitchen, which she was sure would have lived up to Mother's predictions of being warm and cozy in spite of the coldest of winter days. When we got there we saw that the wind had blown the papers out of the cracks in the wall. We couldn't see out the windows for frost, and the Findlay Oval had long since given up.

In the main kitchen the wash basin which had been filled the night before was a solid block of ice. Even the water in the kettle was frozen. Father said it would take a week to thaw out the house. He had his bearskin coat over his long underwear, and his breath curled out of his mouth like smoke from a pipe. He kept saying over and over again, "Some people just have to learn the hard way."

There was no time that day for frivolity. With mitts and hats the boys and Father dismantled the stovepipes. There was no mention of giving them their coat of paint. Planks were laid on top of four logs, and the big iron stove heaved on top. It didn't take long to roll it the few feet into the kitchen. It took longer to feel any benefit from the raging fire Father got going once the stove was put together. By that night, the old log house was cozy and warm and the summer kitchen closed for the winter.

The Family Herald and Weekly Star

There wasn't much in the way of amusements on the farm back in the 1930s, but the lack of a radio, or electricity for that matter, didn't stop our family from making its own entertainment . . . sometimes with outside help.

There is no arguing that Eaton's catalogue gave us many hours of entertainment . . . sitting around the old pine table on a winter's night, there wasn't any better way to while away the hours. But I think now, right up there in importance was a wonderful publication that came out every two weeks and found its way to our farm out in Renfrew County. It always came on the same day . . . the mails were more predictable then . . . and we would rush home from school, knowing that it had been delivered right to our mailbox. Ahead of us was a wonderful evening of reading and clipping.

The paper was the *Family Herald and Weekly Star*, and there was something in it for everyone in our family. The night it arrived we would hurry with redding up the kitchen, because the table would have to be cleared and the oilcloth washed and then dried with the tea towel before Mother would let us spread out the paper. Heaven forbid that a crumb or a drop of milk should mar its pages.

It was always Mother's duty to dole out the paper. Father, of course, got the farm section, which I thought then made up the bulk of the paper. Audrey wanted the pen pal section with the letters in it. She often wrote in the hope that one of her letters would be printed. I don't recall that she was ever so fortunate, which gave her great concern, since her friend Iva had her letters printed not once but twice. This led Audrey to comment that she didn't give two hoots in Halifax for the silly *Family Herald and Weekly Star* anyway . . . and she would threaten to never cast her eyes on it again as long as she lived. But of course that threat would last only until the next issue arrived.

Mother loved the fiction story and the recipe page, and there was always a pattern which you could send for if you had the ten cents to do so.

Occasionally Mother would clip out the offer and send off a dime right in an envelope, and within days the pattern would arrive. She would use the same pattern over and over again with different materials. I remember a bloomer pattern she sent for one winter, and my sister Audrey and I thought they were the ugliest things we had ever witnessed in our lives—big voluminous legs, and wide elastic in the waist. But we had to wear them . . . heaven forbid that we should waste a bit of beached flourbag just because we didn't like the look of the bloomers.

My brothers liked the comics, which we never called comics back in the 1930s. They were the funnies. And there was usually a glorious argument over who was going to get the funnies page first.

My favourite part of the paper was the puzzle page. Sometimes it was on the back of the funnies, which presented a problem. Then Mother would have my sister Audrey read me one of the stories found elsewhere in the *Herald*, which didn't please Audrey one bit, but kept me pacified for the time being.

The puzzle page was a delight for a child of the 1930s. There were also pictures to colour with crayons, and word games which could keep me amused for hours.

And when we had had our fill of the *Family Herald and Weekly Star*, Mother would gather up the pages and put them all back in order. She would take her best cutting scissors and spread the paper out before her at the end of the kitchen table. Then she would go through it page by page and scissor everything that caught her fancy.

Father always said when Mother was finished attacking the

Family Herald and Weekly Star there wasn't enough left to put under the kindling in the morning. All these clippings were pasted into big scrapbooks according to subject, and they became our reference books for years to come.

I have no idea today how much a subscription to the paper cost back in the 1930s. I do know that, like us, everyone around us was poor and suffering through the Depression. But when there was no money for new shoe laces, or an ice cream cone at Briscoe's General Store, there was always money to renew our subscription to the *Family Herald and Weekly Star*.

When I think today of the pleasure it brought to our whole family, I believe it was probably one of the better bargains of those Depression years.

Mother's Bribe

It was one of those winters in the 1930s when Father was able to find a day or two of work back in the bush hauling logs for a big Ottawa lumber camp. The meagre pay helped augment what little income we managed to stimulate during the long cold months.

It was while Father was away, often for several days at a time, that Mother got the urge to make some changes in our old log house, modifications which she knew perfectly well would not sit well with Father had he been home.

So it was that on a blistering cold Friday night, after we had done the chores and put a big log on the cookstove, Mother announced we were going to make a big change in the parlour in the morning. A neighbour had come around to tell Mother that Father would be working in the bush until the first of the next week, and Mother sounded almost relieved.

She said we were going to tear up the oilcloth on the parlour floor. Audrey and I sucked in our breath and Emerson said, "Holy Smoke." It was Everett who reminded Mother that Father said the oilcloth had been there when he was a little boy, and as far as he was concerned it was good for another hundred years.

It was the *colour* that Mother hated. It was dark blue, and looked as if it had been painted, and then sponged over with a light brown colour, making it look as if someone had spilled gravy and not bothered to wipe it up.

We reminded Mother that Father had made quite an issue the last time Mother said she was going to rip up the oilcloth. We might as well have saved our breath. Mother had made up her mind and that's all there was to it. The oilcloth was coming off!

She sent Everett to the drive shed for two claw hammers to lift the carpet tacks, and she explained she was going to roll it up and put it in the back shed just in case she wanted to put it down in the summer kitchen come spring. "Although I doubt I will ever want to see it again," she added, as she attacked the oilcloth with a smart blow of the hammer.

We were not too surprised to see that underneath the oilcloth were old copies of the *Renfrew Mercury*. Earl was told to gather them up and feed them into the stove, pulling them out from under the oilcloth as she worked. Everett and Emerson were instructed to roll up the oilcloth as it was loosened.

It wasn't a big parlour, and so within an hour the floor was naked, except for another layer of papers that seemed to be stuck to the floor. The brothers carried the roll of oilcloth to the back shed.

We all got down on our hands and knees and picked away at the papers, using kitchen knives. We hadn't gone very far when Mother raised her hand, indicating that we were to stop. She was looking under the bottom layer of papers. And there was the worst-looking floor any of us had ever seen. It wasn't even the same as the rest of the floors in the house, and certainly not at all like the rest of the parlour. It looked like a patch-work quilt. Tiny little pieces of flooring joined longer strips, and in some places gouges convinced me we would probably be able to see clear down to the cellar when the last bit of paper was pulled off. It was obvious that our ancestors had never finished putting down a proper floor in the first place.

Mother sent Emerson and Everett to the shed for the old oil-cloth and told them to hurry. Audrey and I were ordered to the woodbox to get an armful of *Renfrew Mercury*s. I said Father would sure be surprised when we told him what we had found under the carpet. Mother said there was no need in the world to mention a word to Father.

We all stopped and looked at Mother down on her knees spreading *Renfrew Mercury*s. I said I thought Father would be real interested. "I'll bet he would," Emerson added. Without looking up Mother said, "How would you all like to go to the picture show tomorrow night in Renfrew?" Audrey was ecstatic. Janet Gaynor was playing in "Tess of the Storm Country," and she was dying to see it. "Then it's settled," Mother said. We knew exactly what she meant. Father was not to hear about the oilcloth.

Today, this would be called bribing your children. Back then, we preferred to think of it as a simple negotiation which in the long run would save us all from a family argument when Father got home from the bush.

The Christmas Box

Excitement always ran high on our farm in Renfrew County at Christmas time. A scant array of presents and little money for extras never dampened the holiday spirit that prevailed in our old log house. What did cause us concern, one year, was the lack of that call from the stationmaster at the CPR station in Renfrew.

The Christmas box arrived from Chicago every year. It was the difference between having a meagre Christmas, or one filled with excitement. Aunt Freda was Father's spinster sister. We thought she must surely be very rich to live in a place like Chicago. She was also a sister to Aunt Lizzie in Regina, who twice a year sent us the hand-me-down boxes filled with her two sons' outgrown clothes. Aunt Lizzie never sent us anything for Christmas. But Aunt Freda always packed a box of unbelievable treasures and it came by train. We knew it had arrived when the stationmaster would phone and say, "That box is here." We knew exactly what he meant. We would be filled with such excitement we could barely contain ourselves, and we would beg Father to let us go into Renfrew with him on the sleigh to get it.

But it was only a few days before Christmas, and there was still no call from the station. The *Ottawa Farm Journal* had been full of terrible stories on the Depression—how it had hit the entire world, even places like Chicago. So maybe there wasn't to be a parcel from Aunt Freda that year after all.

After school had been let out for the holidays, we would run into the house several times a day to ask Mother if there had been any important phone calls. She always said, "No. Not yet." And she tried to tell us gently that the call might not come this year at all. After all, the Chicago parcel always arrived a couple of weeks before Christmas.

We tried to envision what Christmas would be like without Aunt Freda's gifts. The year before I had received a beautiful book with coloured pictures . . . my very first. Aunt Freda had sent the prettiest blouse I had ever seen, all ribbons at the neck with puffy sleeves and clear glass buttons down the front. I had never had anything with clear glass buttons before.

Now it was just three days before Christmas, and still no call from the stationmaster in Renfrew. Mother tried to tell us that we should remember the true meaning of Christmas . . . that it was Jesus' birth we should be thinking about. But I'm afraid her lecture was lost on five young children from the backwoods of Renfrew County.

At night I asked Audrey if she thought it was a sin to pray for the box to arrive. She said she hoped it wasn't because she had been praying for it for more than a week. And so in bed when the lamp had been blown out, and we were in the solitude of our own room, we prayed silently that the call would come before it was too late.

The day before Christmas broke clear and cold. Mother was going about the business of preparing as much of the dinner as possible, so that Christmas day could be spent at church functions and singing, and welcoming visitors from the community.

We five youngsters, I must admit, felt we had been robbed. The telephone rang many times that morning. But always the calls were from a neighbour. At the noon meal Father looked around the table and gently explained that it wouldn't matter if the call came anyway; it was too late to drive twelve miles into Renfrew to get the parcel. It would be pitch black by the time we made it back with the horses and sleigh. A heavy gloom settled over us children. Again we got the lecture on the true meaning of Christmas.

The phone rang just as Father was taking his last gulp of noon-hour tea. It gave out our ring twice before anyone moved to answer it. Mother took the receiver off the hook and we heard her say hello to Mr. Briscoe from the General Store. The gloom deepened.

It wasn't the long-awaited call from the stationmaster. She wished him a merry Christmas and thanked him for his call.

When Mother turned from the phone on the wall, she was beaming. "It has arrived at Briscoe's General Store. Someone was in the station when it came on the morning train. They knew it was a Christmas box, and brought it out to the store. We can pick it up there."

We tore away from the table with Father saying, "Hold it, hold it; we don't all have to go." But his words were wasted on us. We were in our clothers in jig time, and Everett had the horses hitched and at the back door in minutes for the three-mile ride to the general store. We sang all the way there and all the way back. We sang in joy . . . and with a new sense of the true meaning of Christmas, I thought. We took turns sitting with our arms around the box to hold it on the flat-bottomed sleigh. It was a joyous day . . . the sun was shining . . . fresh snow had fallen through the night . . . the air was crisp and cold . . . it was going to be a wonderful Christmas after all. ▬

Christmas Traditions

Christmas baking filled most of the month of December. Father couldn't understand what all the fuss was about, or why Mother made cake tin after cake tin of treats. He said we had no more company at Christmas time than we had at any other time of the year, and to squirrel away cookies, small cakes, tarts, and loaves was just a waste of time and energy, not to mention the cost.

Mother, of course, paid him no heed. What did a man know about what was needed at the Christmas season? And so the days were filled with baking, and the evenings spent on making icings and fillings for cakes. We seemed to have an abundance of cookie tins in those days, and they were lined with brown paper, filled to the lids, and put out in the summer kitchen to await the guests Mother anticipated every year, and whom Father said would never come.

They were both partly right. Mother always made far too much and expected many more drop-in visitors than came. But at Christmas time we saw neighbours we hadn't seen since winter began, and even though Father never expected them, he was always delighted when they appeared at our back door.

Mother's specialties were pork pie and butter tarts. By mid-December, she would start talking about the big job which lay ahead. Father said if it was so much work, why did she bother. But she said it just wouldn't be Christmas without tourtière and butter tarts. She made them both on the same day, using the same rich French pastry for both crusts. She would grind pork in the big meat grinder that attached to the edge of the table, simmer it down with garlic cloves and cinnamon, add a bit of cornstarch to thicken, and continue cooking until it was like a fine porridge.

The butter tart fillings were made without raisins or currants . . . just lots of corn syrup and butter and fresh eggs, and both the pork pies and tarts would be popped into the big Findlay Oval at the same time. Mother always made these specialties on a Saturday so that my sister Audrey and I would learn how to master them as well.

We expected Father to come in to his mid-day dinner complaining about the nonsense of baking so much when the cost of the ingredients was so high. He'd mumble a bit in German and take off his work coat and hat with the fur ear lugs and hang them on the peg at the back door. His routine never changed. He'd wash his hands in the basin of clean water on the bench and dry them on the huck towel. And then he would walk over to the reservoir of the Findlay Oval and place the bowl of his pipe on the lid, leaving the stem to hang over the edge. He would walk over to the old pine table with the red and white checked oilcloth on it and sit down at the head of the table. As like as not Mother would be humming Christmas carols in the background. She would put a plate of steaming hot vittles in front of Father, who would take not more than a second to scan the plate. And always there would be a big slab of tourtière, the French pork pie Father insisted was not necessary and an extravagance. Beside his plate Mother would have put a nappy of homemade chili sauce, because Father liked chili sauce on everything but dessert.

After a meaningful grace Father would polish off his dinner with great gusto and then hand the empty plate to Mother, indicating he was ready for another helping.

By the time he was finished there wouldn't be enough of the tourtière left on the pie plate to fill a corn cob pipe. And he'd have no trouble working his way through three or four butter tarts washed down with a few cups of green tea.

It always took that first meal of pork pie and butter tarts to bring Father around to Mother's way of thinking about preparing for Christmas. And before the weekend was over, Father himself would be making one or two of his own German specialties to add to the ever growing pile of treats in the freezing summer kitchen. And no one enjoyed visits from the neighbours more than Father during that Christmas season. He would always head right out to the lean-to, coming in with an armful of cookie tins, ready and more than willing to share the season's bounty.

The Christmas Concert

School Christmas concerts were supposed to bring joy, but for me, more often than not, they were a time of embarrassment and pain. I was a shy child, the youngest in the Northcote school, and I lived in the shadow of the schoolmate whose mission in life was to cause me misery and anguish.

Marguerite excelled at the Christmas concert. Outgoing, with bouncing golden curls and clothes bought from Eaton's catalogue, Marguerite was usually the Virgin Mary, and I, as often as not, was a sheep. I don't think I was ever elevated beyond that status all the time I went to the Northcote school. I was always a sheep.

Everyone got dressed up in their Sunday best for the Christmas concerts. The entire community crowded into the little one-room schoolhouse with the roaring fire in the pot-bellied stove belting out an unbelievable heat.

My stomach churned from the time Mother put the big flat ribbon on the top of my head at home until I mounted the makeshift stage and, behind a creton curtain, got down on all fours under a car robe. Miss Crosby fashioned black hooves out of bristol board, and I wore a black toque with buttons sewn on it for eyes. I no more looked like a sheep than a hippopotamus, but it was the best Miss Crosby could do with limited resources.

Marguerite, on the other hand, looked every inch the Virgin Mary. The young junior fourth boy with whom I was secretly in love played Joseph, which gave me still another reason to resent my school enemy.

I remember the year Miss Crosby decided she would spice up the nativity scene a bit by having Mary and Joseph more animated. Mary, instead of a long white dress, was going to wear a short grain sack affair and be in her bare feet. Joseph was to be attired in like fashion. And rather than kneel, the two were to enter from the side, go to the manger, and witness the baby on the mound of hay. At that point, Mary was to raise her hands high over her head and proclaim to all the miracle of the birth. Marguerite was right in her element. As she bounced across the stage and came to a halt in front of the mound of hay, I hissed to Joyce Francis that I was sure the Virgin Mary didn't get *her* curls from the beauty parlour in Renfrew.

All the time this pantomime was going on, the rest of the Northcote school pupils were just off stage singing *Away in a Manger*. My brother Emerson was the horse. He was to make a whinnying noise occasionally, and Joyce and I were to let out well-timed baas when Miss Crosby raised her eyebrows in our direction from behind the curtain.

The lamps had been blown out in the school, but the stage was well lit by three large lanterns. Much later Mother, who was loath to say anything detrimental about anyone, commented that the lighting was most appropriate.

I'm not too sure just when all hell broke loose. But chaos came suddenly and without warning. Marguerite had come to a halt in front of the hay. She glared at the gathering of pupils who were singing in the background. If she was going to speak, she wanted no opposition. Miss Crosby motioned with her hand to quieten everyone down, and then she nodded in Marguerite's direction. Joyce and I baaed, and Emerson whinnied. Marguerite turned to the audience, making sure she wasn't hidden by Joseph.

She raised her arms high in the air and, just as she turned her eyes to the ceiling for the most dramatic impact, her underwear fell from her waist and settled around her bare feet.

The choir abruptly stopped singing; Joseph, who was standing slightly behind Marguerite, slapped his thigh and started to roar; and Miss Crosby struggled frantically with the creton curtain to get it to close.

She hustled the choir to the front of the stage and commanded them to sing. The audience had the common sense to sit still and wait for the next number. As for Marguerite, she dissolved into tears, and was too overcome to even stoop down and pick up her store-bought underwear.

It would be nice to say the whole episode was forgotten. But like all school children of any era, there was always someone around to remind Marguerite of that fateful Christmas concert when she lost her underwear at centre stage. I don't think she was ever the Virgin Mary again. The plum role was given to another girl, whose girth guaranteed her underwear would stay intact. As for me, I remained a reluctant sheep all the years I went to the Northcote school. ⪻

Father's New Robe

We thought Aunt Freda was a little strange. She was the youngest of Father's sisters and she had moved to Chicago when she was barely into her twenties. No one in Northcote saw or heard of her much after that. But once or twice a year a parcel would come, covered with American stamps, wrapped in plain brown paper and tied with heavy cord. The gifts were almost like a puzzle; sometimes it took us a very long time to figure out why Aunt Freda would send what she did. Very seldom was there a note of explanation . . . just the parcel.

That's what happened one day when the snow was piled high against the side of the old log house and the mailman had a dickens of a time getting down the Northcote side road because of drifts. The mailbox was turned towards the road, which meant there was mail inside.

It was a soft parcel . . . felt like clothes, Audrey said, always hopeful that Aunt Freda would send her something pretty from one of those big American department stores we heard about. It was addressed to Father, but that in itself wasn't strange, because everything Aunt Freda sent us, including her letters, were addressed to Father. Audrey was still holding out hope that it would be a dress for her. Mother cut the string with the butcher knife, and inside was a piece of notepaper that said "Happy Birthday Albert." Father's birthday was months away. "Just like Freda," Mother said. There was a parcel wrapped in white tissure paper, and Mother handed it over to Father, who would much rather be reading the *Ottawa Farm Journal* than opening up a parcel that he was sure would be of no earthly use to him.

And there inside was a kimono. A sort of fuzzy plaid material, with a braided cord running around the collar and a rope belt. Father held it up to the coal oil lamp. "What in tarnation is that?" he asked. "It's a man's kimono," Mother offered. Father turned the thing around in his hand. "And what, may I ask, is a kimono?"

"You wear it at night before going to bed, or if you have to get up to light the fire . . . or go outside to the privy." Mother was losing her patience over Father's unworldliness. Father kept turning it over in his hand. Emerson suggested if he didn't want it, maybe one of the boys could have it . . . they could pull straws for it. Father, it was obvious, had no intention of parting with whatever it was his sister had sent him, and he got out of his chair and walked to the bedroom to tuck it away.

The kimono was all but forgotten until one Saturday night when Mother had invited some of the neighbours in for a game of euchre. It was a typical cold winter's night. The logs of the house were crackling and the cookstove was revved up as far as it would go. We children had washed up and changed from our play clothes to our next-to-Sunday best. Mother was in a clean housedress with a freshly starched pinny on top. Father had yet to make a move from the rocker by the stove. Mother pointed to the gingerbread clock to remind him the Thoms and Hineses would be there any minute. He lumbered out of the rocker and sauntered into the bedroom off the kitchen, emerging a few minutes later, just as we heard a knock at the back door. There he was, fully dressed . . . wool pants that he had worn all day, his plaid shirt and his grey work socks, and over everything was the plaid kimono. Mother just looked at him. Even I knew what a kimono was for, and it wasn't for wearing over your clothes when you had company. But it was too late—Uncle Alec Thom and Aunt Bertha were already in the kitchen and the Hineses weren't far behind. Father went right to the door and stretched out his hand in welcome. If anyone wondered what a man was doing in his kimono, fully clothed underneath, no one said a word, and Mother made no apology, as if being so attired for company on a Saturday night was perfectly normal.

I sat close by Father during the euchre game and occasionally I would run my hand over the sleeve of the kimono. It smelled like brand new flannelette, and as the evening wore on, I began to think Father looked almost like one of those businessmen from Renfrew. Important-like. Neither Alec Thom nor Jimmy Hines mentioned the kimono, but I could see them looking at it, and I daresay they wondered how a farmer of such modest means could come up with such an elegant piece of clothing.

Ronny on the River

It was always exciting when the Montreal cousins stayed on after the Christmas holidays. I especially enjoyed it, since cousin Ronny was close to me in age. But Ronny, being Ronny, always managed to cause a stir in our household.

It was a snapper of a day that Sunday in January. A good old-fashioned winter with lots of snow and so cold that frost formed on our scarves pulled up over our mouths. It was the kind of day I loved. After church we bundled up in our heaviest clothes, put on our skates and headed for the frozen Bonnechere.

Ronny had spanking new skates. I had to content myself with runners which fastened onto my galoshes with leather straps. But it was the joy of being out with my brothers, sister, cousins, and the neighbour children that thrilled me. And even though I hated the old runner skates, I hated missing skating more.

My three brothers had shovelled off a section of the river, and it was as clear as glass and crackled under our weight. When we reached the river bank we could see the Thom children heading over from the next farm. It was going to be a wonderful afternoon.

Ronny took to the ice as if he was born on it. He said he skated on a real rink in Montreal, and he made it clear that the cleaned-off Bonnechere left a lot to be desired. He stumbled a few times on the cracks, and I could tell he was concerned that his performance would appear to be less than perfect. Ronny never liked to be anything but the best.

All the Thom children had arrived and were sitting on the old fallen maple tree to put on their skates. We waved and beckoned them to hurry. It was always more fun when the cleared-off ice was packed with skaters. But Ronny had other plans. He skated over to the tree and asked Leo, the oldest Thom boy, where he planned on skating. Leo ignored him. Ronny worked down the line of Thoms and didn't get much more of a response than he did from Leo.

"Well, you certainly can't skate here," Ronny announced. "This part of the Bonnechere belongs to us." Leo looked up from his skates. "Nobody owns the river, you city slicker," he said. Well, there was nothing Ronny liked more than a good scrap. And even though Leo was twice his size, Ronny began pulling on his ankles, which were dangling from the fallen maple tree. Leo was off the tree in a flash and took off after Ronny, who was heading out to the patch of ice with his head down and his scarf blowing out like a flag in the wind. Leo didn't even have his boots on . . . just his heavy grey hand-knit socks. Of course, he didn't have a hope of catching the young rascal from Montreal. Ronny kept yelling insults over his shoulder and Leo was still bent on catching up with him.

I was watching the whole performance from the sidelines and wondering where cousin Ronny got the gall to announce who could and could not skate on the Bonnechere. He was a spunky one all right. Finally, Leo figured out that the only thing he was going to get from the chase was frozen feet, and he headed back to the tree to put on his skates. As soon as Ronny saw that he wasn't going to get any more reaction from Leo, he set his sights on another of the family, my little friend Velma, and began telling her that that portion of the Bonnechere was Haneman property, and suggested she skate on the part of the river that ran in front of *their* house. Finally my sister Audrey had to intervene and told Ronny to hush up or our mother would be sent for and she would settle his hash once and for all. He sulked for the rest of the afternoon.

As always, someone hitched up a team of horses to the old flat-bottomed sleigh and came to fetch us home. We would be half frozen to death and our ankles would be aching like fury. This day we saw Uncle Alec Thom coming across the field. We never bothered to take off our skates . . . we clutched our boots and fell onto the sleigh. And that was when the second fight of the day began.

The Thom children wouldn't let Ronny on the sleigh. They said he didn't own it. It was Thom property. Ronny looked to Emerson for support, but Emerson just shrugged his shoulders. Everett pretended to be untying knots in his skates. The sleigh was pulling away from the bank of the river, and Ronny was standing knee-deep in snow with his skates on contemplating his next move.

He started running in his skates, his chunky legs trying to keep up, but he quickly fell behind. When he did catch hold there was a Thom there to push him off. Finally Uncle Alec brought the sleigh to a halt and the young cousin, panting for breath, was allowed to crawl on. Three big strapping Thom boys lined up behind him. "Who owns the Bonnechere, Ronny?" one asked.

Ronny surveyed the situation. He wasn't going to answer—that was plain to see. Leo put his skates to Ronny's back ready to push him off. Ronny looked at the long lane home and the darkening sky. He shrugged. "Everybody, I guess," he mumbled.

Farm Riches

Back in the 1930s, intensely cold weather was normal. We expected it and rarely were we disappointed. I can remember the landscape being one solid mass of white crust, glistening in the sun, and sparkling like a million diamonds on a moonlit night. I can still see how the Northcote side road met the fields like a white sea, with no suggestion of ditches, and fences completely hidden from view.

It was often so bitterly cold that we went to school with nothing but our eyes showing . . . with heavy wool scarves completely circling our heads and tucked into the necks of our coats. More often than not, a pair of men's socks covered our hands and went right up our arms, followed by two pair of heavy hand-knit mittens. Our feet were tucked into galoshes with felt inner soles, and buckles fitted tightly around our legs to keep out the snow.

None of us complained much. Father always said there wasn't one thing we could do about the weather. And so we struggled on, one day after another, waiting for a January thaw that, as often as not, never arrived.

But there was a pause in this intense cold that had nothing to do with the outside elements. And that pause came for me in the evening just before Mother would announce that it was almost time for bed.

The last thing Father did every winter night of his life before he bade us goodnight and we headed up the stairs, was light the lantern that hung at the back door. I would watch his every move waiting for the signal. He would, I thought, take the longest time. First he would pack a bowl of tobacco into his pipe, tap it down, and light it from a sliver of wood ignited in the cookstove.

Why didn't he hurry, I would wonder. As he reached for his big work jacket with the plaid lining, he would look over at me and ask, "Well?" That was the word I waited for. I would dart from the kitchen table and grab my outdoor clothes and hurriedly cram my feet into my galoshes. Father would take the lit lantern off the bench and open the door to the bitterly cold winter night. There would be only a narrow path to the barn, just room for one person at a time. Father would walk ahead as a windbreak, and I would follow close behind.

We would start in the cow byre. It led directly into the main barn where the horses and sheep were kept. And I would feel the most delicious warmth as we closed the small door cut out of the big door like a postage stamp. The lantern gave off just enough light to see where we were walking. Father would go to the heads of the cattle and make sure they had feed for the night and that each one was secure. Always one or two would make sounds of recognition, and he would make soothing noises, and sometimes he would rub their heads between their ears.

Then we would head into the part of the barn that housed the horses and the sheep. Here there was a sweeter smell, and the sheep would let us know they were there by rushing to the edge of their pens waiting for the bit of feed Father would toss into their pails.

The horses, some of them lying down on the soft straw, would whinny, and Father and I would make sure they were well bedded down for the night. I would feel the utmost contentment. I would look over the farm animals, and think how wonderful it was to be so rich. Well, didn't we have a barn full of livestock? Wasn't there a hay mow full of feed, and bins full of grain? What was all this talk about a Depression? Surely it was happening someplace else. I wouldn't allow myself to think of the Saturday trips into town to barter for our supplies, or the hand-me-down box that kept clothes on our backs, or the countless times Mother said, "don't you know there is a Depression on?" When I was with Father as he checked our livestock every night, the winter could be raging outside, and the drifts as high as our window sills—the Depression was the farthest thing from my mind. I was safe, and filled with gratitude for my happy rich life. At that special time, the Depression was not part of my existence. It belonged to someone else.

Sliding Down Hill

The west hill was like a white shiny mountain. The week before, sleet and snow had covered it and formed a hard crust. As I looked at it out the kitchen window I thought it belonged in a picture book. And now it was Sunday. We had done our chores, gone to church, and changed into our play clothes, and I could hardly stand the excitement, knowing what was ahead.

We were going to the west hill to slide. Saturday, Mother had brought home huge cardboard boxes from town and they would be our toboggans. Everett said our homemade sleighs would cut right through the crust on the hill, but the boxes would send us flying down and right across the Bonnechere River.

We were to meet all the Thoms there. They were our neighbours and our best friends, and Leo had called to say he would be bringing his own sleigh . . . the cardboard boxes were fine, but he had something much better to show us. Everett said once again that if Leo thought a sleigh was going to slide down the hill he was in for a great surprise . . . it would be going nowhere.

The Thoms had farther to go than we did, what with the west hill being on our property. It took us forever to climb the hill because of the glare ice and crust, but we finally made it to the top. Everett positioned the boxes and said we could probably all have a run before the Thoms got there. And so Audrey and I climbed into a box and Everett gave us a mighty shove. My heart stood still as we careened down the hill. Only Audrey could see where we were heading. We glided to a stop and rolled out of the box laughing so hard I didn't think I would ever make it back up to the top.

And there were the Thoms, struggling up the hill on the other side. Leo was dragging something behind him that certainly wasn't familiar to either Audrey or me. It looked like a huge shovel . . . or curved metal . . . Audrey said he probably made it. But when he got closer we could see it was the shiny fender off a car.

We all begged to have a turn, but Leo said it would go far too fast for the girls, and just the boys would get to ride it down the hill.

There it sat like a big gravy boat. Audrey and Iva were positioned at either end to hold it straight, and about four boys climbed onto it. Those that were left on the hill were ordered to shove with all their might and the big black fender took off down the hill like a bullet. There was no doubt it was a wonderful invention.

It was quite a chore to keep it upright, but with so many boys in its curve, they were able to keep it going in a straight line. I thought at the time I had never seen everyone have such a grand time.

Alas, the fun was short-lived. Audrey saw Uncle Alec first. Our family called him Uncle Alec, although he really was no relation, but he was the Thom children's father and we knew him as well as we knew our own parents. He was tearing across the field like a rabbit, heading right for the west hill. Every step he took saw him go up to his waist in the snow, right through the crust. The closer he got to the hill the clearer we saw that he wasn't coming to join in the fun.

His face was beet red even though it was a cold and windy day. The boys didn't see him immediately because they were still at the bottom of the hill trying to lug the car fender back to the top. Leo saw him first, and he stopped dead in his tracks. Uncle Alec grabbed one of the big cardboard boxes, climbed inside and ordered Iva to push-start him. He went down the hill like an arrow, sailed right by the boys and came to a halt, banged up against a tree, which did little for his disposition.

We could hear him roar all the way from the top of the west hill. What we couldn't understand, Iva was only too willing to fill in for us. It seems that wasn't an *old* fender at all. Uncle Alec had taken it off the car in his drive shed to make repairs to the Ford, which at that very minute was up on blocks for the winter. Furthermore, he had just painted it. Well, there wasn't much left to the paint job. The last we saw of the Thom boys, they were walking across the field with the fender over their heads like a canoe. Uncle Alec was swishing their legs with a branch he had pulled off the maple. Our day of sliding was over. ___

The Birthday Cake

Birthday parties were considered frivolous, and were reserved for children of wealthy people like Marguerite or my little friend Joyce, both of whom lived in brick houses, not log ones like ours.

Mother, however, made sure our birthdays within the family got as much attention as we could afford. We always got a small book, and we children made each other gifts like felt pencil cases, and we sometimes painted lids on small jars which held things like special buttons or our pennies. And always there was a birthday cake. A square chocolate cake with mile-high white icing.

The most exciting thing to me, even more exciting than having a party, was finding the little treasures Mother put in the cake each birthday. There was always a dime, and several pennies, and little prizes that came in crackerjack boxes. These were wrapped tightly in pieces of waxed paper and cooked right along with the cake.

Then came the year when Mother thought I was old enough to make my own birthday cake. This was certainly a landmark event as far as I was concerned. Audrey and the brothers had been making their birthday cakes for years, but I was always considered too young until that year when I was seven years old.

That year my birthday fell on a Saturday, so I was assured I could make the cake as soon as my house chores were finished in the morning, and we would have the cake for dessert that night.

Mother said I could even wrap the prizes in the waxed paper, and that Audrey would help me when it came time to add them to the batter. I begged Mother to let me do it by myself. After all I was going to be seven, and I was sure I was old enough to handle something as simple as putting paper-wrapped prizes in the cake. I had seen Mother and Audrey do it often enough, goodness knows, sitting with my elbows on the table waiting for the last drop to be poured into the pan so that I could lick the bowl.

Mother propped her recipe against the flour tin and made sure I had everything out on the kitchen table before I started. Then she and Audrey went to the barns to help with the chores. Never had I felt so grown-up. Mother had put a good-sized log in the stove and the Findlay Oval was fair jumping by the time I added the last egg to the bowl.

I had the little prizes wrapped . . . all twisted inside small pieces of waxed paper. I poured the batter into the cake pan, and scooping up the prizes in one hand, dumped them into the cake all at once. They sank like stones.

I pulled a chair up to the Findlay Oval, and sat looking at the gingerbread clock. Mother said it would take half an hour to cook.

I yanked a straw from the broom when the time was up and it came out of the cake as clean as a whistle. My beautiful cake was done.

After the noon meal Mother helped me beat the icing, and the cake by then was cool to the touch. I could hardly wait until supper. Father said it was the nicest cake he had ever seen. I was feeling particularly benevolent, and even though I had hoped to get at least the dime in my piece of cake, I hoped that everyone at the table would get a treasure. The first thing I did was break my portion with my spoon. There was nothing there. Audrey found nothing either . . . nor did Mother or Father.

What could have happened? I knew I put them in the batter. I remember dropping the whole handful in at once when the cake was in the pan. And then Emerson let out a war whoop that could be heard in Admaston. There on his plate was every wrapped surprise I had added to the cake, all in one piece. I couldn't understand it.

Mother asked me if I had spaced the pieces out in the batter. Of course I hadn't. Wasn't the cooking supposed to take care of that? Mother said no, the prizes had to be separated in the cake tin.

Well, there was Emerson refusing to give up one surprise. He got them fair and square, he said, and he wasn't about to part with a thing. I started to cry. Emerson ran to the parlour with his plate, Audrey began to call him names, and Mother was at the blue jug at the cupboard trying to find a few pennies to give to the losers. Over the din Father was heard to say, "Can't a man have his supper in peace after a hard day's work any more?"